TOUCHING ALL BASES

Jerry Bocian

AuthorHouse™
1663 Liberty Drive, Suite 200
Bloomington, IN 47403
www.authorhouse.com
Phone: 1-800-839-8640

© 2009 Jerry Bocian. All rights reserved.

No part of this book may be reproduced, stored in a retrieval system, or transmitted by any means without the written permission of the author.

First published by AuthorHouse 2/27/2009

ISBN: 978-1-4389-4441-8 (sc)

Printed in the United States of America
Bloomington, Indiana

This book is printed on acid-free paper.

TOUCHING ALL BASES

    Though the title has baseball connotations, it also pertains to other phases of my life, such as music, travel, religion & navy.

    I wrote this book as if speaking to you, the reader, for a more personal and direct touch, in hopes you will fully understand the gifts of my life. I was truly blessed, and I realize it. My greatest blessings were my children and my wife, Kay. They all had a hand in the editing of this book, plus reminding me of certain memories I might have otherwise forgotten.

PROLOGUE

I was born a "poor but rich" Polish child on the south side of Chicago in the shadow of the steel mills. I was christened Gerald Francis Bocian. After many childhood fights with my beloved sisters and many so-called "friends," the "Gerald" was dropped and I became thereafter and forever known as Jerry. I never told ANYBODY my middle name was Francis. This is my story.

IN THE BEGINNING

One hot, humid, beautiful sunny day, at our beloved Bessemer Park on the far south side of Chicago, our gang was playing a baseball game amongst ourselves. This was in August, 1942. Suddenly, a camera crew appeared, and a spokesperson approached, making us an offer we could not refuse. He offered to take us to Comiskey Park to see the Red Sox play the White Sox, give us all the hot dogs we could eat and sodas to drink. All he wanted in return was to film some of our game and film us at the Sox game. Why? The spokesperson was Lew Fonseca, contracted by the American League to make a documentary on baseball to try to stimulate more interest in our national pastime. This was a much-needed effort as World War II was under way and the depression was in the not too distant past. People simply didn't have money for such a thing as a spectator sport like baseball. After the big day was over, Mr. Fonseca told us the name of his film would be <u>TOUCHING ALL BASES</u>.

I was an honor student at my high school, St. Leo, and took my Dad to school for a father-son evening, where the film was to be shown. Imagine the reaction I got from my fellow students when I told them that I was in the movie. After it was over, I could have told them I would be the next president and they would have believed me. Yes, Dad was surprised. This meeting was about as close as the two of us ever were. I have many regrets to this day about what I would do differently in regards to our relationship. Dad was a patient man; he had to be to put up with his only son. Why he didn't wring my neck is beyond me. When teaching me to tell time, I purposely pretended I didn't get it long after I did. I was with him when he tried to teach mom to drive. Instead of braking when turning a corner, she stepped on the gas. Dad flipped, and mom simply got out of the car, got into the back seat, and never attempted to learn again. That's my Dad (and my Mom).

By the end of the fall season, Dad was hired in at Union Carbide, and so the rest of the story unfolds. I cannot forget about Mom during these troubled times. She was Dad's strength, though always in the background. Her schooling was something else. I may have misunderstood her, but as I recall her words, she skipped from fourth grade to eighth, but then they had her do two years of seventh or eighth. Working for the Illinois Bell Telephone Company, she must have been very sharp. I believe she said she worked there from age 13 or so. She also worked at the Country Club to help keep the family afloat. I can recall our family walking to Grandma's house, a good mile plus, then crossing above the B & O Railroad tracks on the viaduct. Who says we didn't exercise?

Another reason not to forget Mom's input here. When baking pies, she would make one extra crust for me. Also, after my softball games, my team would gather and my sister Dee would have her friends over. We kept the neighborhood awake with singing. Mom would break out her famous SAND PIE (graham cracker crust with applesauce filling).

Until this writing endeavor, it never dawned on me that neither Mom nor Dad ever saw me play any ball games. I must say, though, that Uncle John Rybicki did. We did bowl together at the parish bowling alleys across the street from home. This was a family tradition at any family gathering. My buddies and I were relegated to get the alleys ready for the next bowling season. Mr. Joe Cusick was in charge. His job was driving a steel truck, and invariably he would check on us to see that we were doing our job. Well, we posted one of us to watch out for him, and we would bowl to our hearts' content. We had five of the best pin boy bowlers in the city of Chicago. Some days, we bowled a full season of games. Considering we paid nothing for bowling, it was no wonder that we became pretty sharp at bowling.

About once a month, Father Stanley Dopak would have a priest friend of his come in and they would bowl a few games. Lucky me, I would be called out of class to set pins for them. I looked forward to those days. Father Stanley and I became good friends. In later years, I visited him at a nursing home on Chicago's far north side. He was grateful for the visit and we had an enjoyable hour or so. The next year, I visited him again, in a different home. That visit was uncomfortable. I didn't know what malady he had, but if I moved within two feet of him, he would go into a frenzy, fearing I would touch his feet. His pain must have been unbearable. He had a biological brother (also a priest) he was caring for, who also must have had the same malady before passing away. What happened to the Golden Years? TV commercials belie the true facts about old age. Everything advertised works on TV, but not when you get it home.

When I was about five, I found some money in Mom's purse. Wishing to be the big shot on our block, I proceeded to go to the bowling alley across the street, spent it all on candy and treated all my friends to sweets. This at a time the depression was upon us full tilt.

Mom scrimped and saved and bought me a pair of skates, which I sold and again bought candy to treat my constituents. I must have been dreaming of being a politician. Is it any wonder why I have such a sweet tooth to this day?

Dad had a scheduled Sunday afternoon pinochle game, and asked me to roll him about fifty cigarettes with his new cigarette machine. Sure, Dad, I will be glad to do so. I found the temptation too great, so I proceeded to roll out sixty. With the other ten stashed away, I waited for a clear day when nobody was home, inviting my buddies for a "smoke out." Well, we huffed and puffed and the smoke went out the basement screens. The neighbor thought we were on fire and called the fire department. I thought Dad would skin me alive. What a Dad. All he said was, "I don't care if you smoke, son, just BUY YOUR OWN!" Not ever getting an allowance, that cured me of smoking. I was the only one in my division and on my sub that didn't smoke, and they were free, too.

Dad loved sitting on the back porch on hot nights, enjoying his smoking. My buddies and I opened the garage door (quietly), pushed the car out onto the street, and went for a joyride. Upon return, Dad was still sitting there, so we reversed our movements and thought we really fooled him. NOT SO. The next morning Dad asked me where I went with the car, and I told him. He knew we took it for an extra long ride, and said "Next time put some gas in so I don't run out on the way to work."

Precious moments with Mom in her last days at the hospital. She was coherent, though blind and partially deaf, and in good spirits. We discussed all the changes that took place since she was born. Then we talked about when I sent her and Dad to Florida by plane. Upon return, she talked about "Jerry's plane this," and "Jerry's plane that." At the age of 53 I finally got my pilot's license. Afterward I took my sister Babe up in a small plane for a ride, and on returning home Babe said, "Jerry's plane didn't have any stewardess, nor a toilet, nor cocktails, so don't tell me again about Jerry's plane." Their flight to Florida was their first, and Dad was so engrossed in talking to his seatmate, he never realized that they had a close call on landing at O'Hare, causing them to go around after being almost at touchdown. Mom knew it, but Dad didn't.

On a trip to visit my sister Colette, I planned on dropping Mom off with Colette at her Tampa, Florida home, and continuing on to my Armellini Express meetings in Stuart, Florida (we represented Armellini in Chicago for 40 years). It was mid-winter, and icy conditions throughout Indiana and Ohio caused us to be re-routed via St. Louis. Halfway to St. Louis, I gassed up my car, and wishing to relieve myself, told Mom I wanted to grab a cup of coffee. In two seconds, she whipped out a cup from her food package, including sandwiches and cookies. Well, I had to tell her my needs, knowing she didn't have a urinal in that package of food. She then understood. We later stopped for a meal, and I discovered that I had no wallet. I told Mom I needed money, so she gave me a twenty. We pulled into a dilapidated motel, to find they would not accept credit cards. "Mom, I need more money." "What did you do with the twenty I gave you this morning?" "Mom, I am 53 years old and will not gyp you. Half the restaurant bill was yours, and half the motel bill is yours, okay?"

Mom was infatuated with my new CB, and talked to people along the way. Since we truly were cash broke now, we prevailed upon one of our Armellini truck drivers to stop, borrowing money from him in case of emergency. He was on his way home, and would be reimbursed before we would get there.

Now we were at Colette's and I took off my shoes and grabbed a beer to relax. Mother dearest came in just then, saying "Jerry, you better get some sleep because you have to get up early to drive downstate to your meetings." "Mom, remember me? I am 53 years old."

When I picked her up for the return trip, we loaded up the trunk with freshly plucked grapefruit and oranges. One thing about traveling with Mom, you won't starve. Her goodie bag had enough boiled eggs, sandwiches, etc., for a Boy Scout Troop.

My associations with the priests and sisters of our parish were the highlights of my life. My eighth grade graduating class (1939) began having reunions in about 1964. At our first one, we had an attendance of over 100, and had seven nuns and four priests in attendance. Naturally, the figures kept decreasing as years went by. We met every five years until the last reunion had only seven of us left. We treated our sisters to a limousine ride from Peterson Avenue to South Chicago Heights. I truly miss those reunions.

The Bocian family had a special bond with our good Felicians. Dad always asked when he entered the house whether the nuns needed a ride, as tired as he was after a hard day's work in the steel mills. I had the distinct honor of serving mass for the nuns at their early morning mass. We lived directly across from their convent, so I was never late, despite the very early hour. After taking them for a ride, mostly to the Mother House, Dad would tell them, "If Jerry misbehaves, spank him, and I will spank him also when he gets home."

Some years ago, I was asked to handle a project for our dear Felician Order. One of the Sisters here at the Mother House had an uncle in Detroit who was a retired Master Sergeant from the Army. He wished to do something for the dear Sisters, so he bought them a new Toyota van. I was asked to handle the raffling off of this vehicle. I was given a mailing list, and thousands of envelopes. I then called on my eighth grade graduating class to set up a program to get the show on the road. Shortly, we had a system in place, and after three or four meetings, we had the list covered, ready to mail.

This had been an enormous problem but my ladies from my class of 1939 were up to it. (We also set up reunions which we then continued having every five years.) I bought the stamps, preparing to get this project finalized, only to get the most serious setback of the program. Returns were very slow and it bothered me. It seems the Post Office used by the Felician Order had an enemy who purposely held up sending out the mail. I didn't find this out until too late. Using the mailing permit was definitely cheaper, but we could have garnered a lot more donations by putting the raffle tickets into the people's hands a lot quicker. I was told by some people that they received our solicitations the day of the drawing, and we had finished addressing the envelopes two months before!

As it were, if memory serves me right, the total "take" was only about $35,000. I thought surely it would be over $50,000. My congrats to my class for their hard work, even though we fell far short of my expectations.

Wasn't that a nice gesture for the uncle who donated the auto?

SUBMARINE SERVICE

Christmastime 1942 came, and I asked mom for carfare to go downtown to look for a job. My friends John and Paul Filipiak, Frank Byers and yours truly decided to enlist in some Service. Seemingly, the first recruitment office we came to as a group was the Navy. I went in alone and sheepishly announced my intention to enlist. They welcomed me and I immediately was put into their system, beginning with paperwork, and then the physical, WHICH I FLUNKED because of a bad tooth. I was so sure of passing, and had my acceptance speech all ready for my buddies, or shall I say "chickens," for they flew the coop; when I came out, they were gone. The Navy would not accept me until the bad tooth was taken care of, so I took care of it myself. I took the train back to South Chicago to my family dentist's office, had him pull the tooth, borrowed train fare from him, and returned to the Navy recruiters. They were amazed to see me so soon, bloody mouth and all. Between us we finalized the paperwork, and I was on my way home requiring parental signatures, since I was only 17 at the time.

Now I was getting cold feet. For reasons unknown to me until this day, I pulled the dumbest stunt of all times. I timed my entrance with Dad's arrival at the supper table. Mom asked, "Did you get a job?" and I said "Yes, $21.00 a month", laid the Navy file in front of her, and ran out of the house like a scared rabbit. I then roamed the streets till almost midnight. There I was, across the street from home, in the darkness, not knowing what I was going to do next, when Mom called from the front porch, "You need to get some sleep, son." Boy, did I ever. My bedroom was adjacent to the kitchen so I overheard Dad saying, "I'll sign for him if he wants to go." That proved to me what a dumb stunt I really pulled. The next day he took me to his lawyer friend, had the papers notarized, and there I was, Navy property for the next four years. WHAT A DAD. How lucky was I to have such an understanding Father and Mother.

Before I go any further, I will give a brief summary of my entire time with the Navy, to put things in perspective. I became Navy property officially on January 2, 1943, after getting my paperwork notarized. I then spent three months in boot camp and two months in fire control school after choosing submarine duty, both at Great Lakes Naval Base north of Chicago. After a seven-day train trip to Keyport, Washington, I trained on torpedoes for three months. I was then sent to San Diego for training on various subs. While awaiting the arrival of the submarine S44 which was coming off patrol in Alaskan waters, to which I was to be assigned, I was returned to Keyport for further torpedo training. Unfortunately for S44, she never returned from patrol, lost with all hands on board.

I was sent on the troop ship Mooremacport to my "permanent" station in Hawaii. I was placed into Sub Division 41 at Pearl Harbor, and, during the next few years, Divisions 42 and 43; my assignment was the training of new personnel on various subs. On July 4, 1944, the S28 was training new personnel out of Pearl Harbor and I was to begin training newcomers that day, but I was also playing softball for the Navy at the same time, and that day our team had a championship (fast-pitch) softball game so they found a substitute for me on the S28. LUCKY ME. S28 went out twenty miles and sunk, never to be heard from again.

The last sub I served on was the USS 236 Silversides. In March of 1945, our patrol area was just off the coast of Japan on air-sea rescue, as the final bombing strikes at the Japanese began. On July 22, a pilot was coming toward us with his controls shot out. He ditched his P51 and we sped toward him. Lt. James Hinkle was happy to see us, needless to say. On July 24, a Hellcat pilot also lost his controls, and Lt. B. V. Burtch was also welcomed on board.

We then headed for Guam for R&R. Just about then the atom bomb finalized the war in no uncertain terms, and we really relished those restful days. The return trip to the USA was painfully slow, for they had us on less than half fuel supply so that they could get all the troops back home. It took us almost six weeks to get to Staten Island via the Panama Canal, and, eventually, to the sub base in New London, Connecticut.

It was there at New London that I truly got my baseball dream into focus. I was asked to play for the base, and one of my teammates was none other than Yogi Berra. One day, after we played six to ten games, he was whisked away to the Yankee Spring Training. One of their top brass liked what he saw in me, and offered me a minor league contract. Instead of getting discharged from Great Lakes, I chose Bainbridge, Maryland, so that I could get to the Yankee office to talk contract. Not having been home for almost four years, I opted to start the following spring. More on baseball to come.

The Silversides eventually followed me to Chicago. We had put her in the mothball fleet in Philadelphia, and the Navy resurrected her for training purposes in Chicago. She was used for training from 1949 until they decided to scrap her in 1970 or so. More about the Silversides follows in another chapter.

I didn't mention my working at the factory at Keyport, mainly because I was shifted into different jobs as needed. All torpedoes had to make three perfect firings before being sent out to the fleet. They would be fired on a range that was a seven-mile straight shot up this natural waterway that almost extended to the naval base at Bremerton, Washington. The torpedoes measured 20 feet 6 inches, weighed approximately 3,400 pounds, with the front three feet filled with water to compensate for the explosives that would fill them when finally sent to the Fleet. After making their run down this channel the water would be expelled and they would bob up and down, awaiting the Navy dive crew which would retrieve them and return them to the factory for corrections. The torpedoes carried three instruments in the heads, which indicated deviations in pitch, depth and roll. With that information, the factory then makes corrections until three perfect runs are shot.

As the torpedo is launched, it settles down to the desired depth, and a man who is stationed on a raft raises a flag to indicate it has passed him and is running true to form. There is a tide factor of about 22 feet, which sometimes curtails the firing of "fish." Sometimes, one too many is fired off, hits bottom, and has its gyro tumble causing it to run amok, changing directions helter-skelter. This has caused many a fisherman to dive off his boat when the "fish" is heading right for him.

Most workers at the factory live in Poulsbo, about seven miles upriver. By car, it is about 20 miles. One night I was placed on shore patrol, and rode the ferry to town. Considering the tide, darkness, and the current, I commended the Captain on his dexterity. I found out that he was blind, and had been doing that for 40 years with his wife right behind him giving instructions. In Hawaii I was kidding a waitress and bet her a coke that I knew where she was from. I won the bet with a lucky guess, doubled it and won again. Not lucky: it was Poulsbo. I had a knack for guessing origins by tone and inflections.

Leaving Keyport, I headed a group of six of us going to San Diego, with fives days' delayed orders. We were all excited about spending five days in Los Angeles. We were living it up, having a sleeper car to ourselves (or so we thought). Somehow, in some way, all our wallets were stolen as we slept. We had to call home for money, which we did, but everything was not lost.

Another Navy man heard of our bad luck, and told me to go to the USO. Talk about a break. We were sent to the Hollywood Guild Canteen, a house paid for and built expressly for those who came to try their luck at fame and didn't make it. Cots to sleep on, a refrigerator full of food and soft drinks, ALL AT NO CHARGE. We were treated to watching the making of two films. One was the "National Barn Dance," and the other was "Holiday on Ice." Back home, I used to listen to the Barn Dance. Lou Costello was in the "Holiday" movie as the ice skating waiter, and he put on a great show. The script called for a waiter on ice skates with the ice rink surrounded by people having lunch under a canopy. The waiter, in addition to carrying a tray full of drinks, skated around the perimeter, knocking down the canopy as he went along, flailing his arms as if he never had skates on before. The director said he expected that scene to take at least ten "takes," but the first was perfect. We were invited to the Costello home where he had a basketball setup, and really showed us what an athlete he truly was. For his roly-poly body, he amazed everybody. We also were invited to the Bing Crosby residence for a few hours. For six forlorn sailors who were penniless coming into Los Angeles just a few short days ago, you couldn't put a price on what we ended up with thanks to the USO.

While training in San Diego, we had another lucky break. One of our group was a look-alike of Bill Bendix. He was asked to be a stand-in, doing the stunts for Bendix in all the Marine war movies. Since we had weekends off, we would get an early start heading for Los Angeles in his car. While he did the stunts, we gawked around, seeing how they fooled the public with cleaver money-saving stunts of their own.

During training in San Diego, I was in the first 20mm gun emplacement of a line of perhaps 12 getting instructions. Since I had never fired a 20mm shot before, I was most interested. Told that every fifth shell was an incendiary, and to use them as visual aids to guide the line of fire towards the target, I was ready to go. As the target approached my emplacement, and given orders to fire, I was leading the incendiaries towards the target, and severed the towing cable. It took a half hour to get another target in line, and I did it again. I was summoned by the Admiral, and asked where I learned to shoot that well. I could have told him from my son Paul, who qualified as an expert rifleman in the Marines, but he wasn't born yet!

With three bucks in my pocket, and payday several days off, I was conned into going to the burlesque show. There I sat, watching ten hefty women playing Christmas songs by jumping up and down with bells hanging from their breasts. It was a wooden stage which shook, as all of San Diego did, I'm certain. My buddies also must have heard me sigh about my last three bucks wasting away, so I left early. They tried to get me to stay, but I left knowing they would come up with some devious plan. Sure enough, almost asleep, I heard them coming not very quietly, calling my name. Fortunately, I had changed bunks and someone else was introduced to the rotten cabbage meant for me. Tom Earley, the ringleader, and I made a pact to visit each other's Mom, whomever got home first. I made it first, and visited Bessie Earley in Brooklyn.

Digressing to a Navy venture in a fire control class. It was in a darkened room, facing a 180 degree stage. Every ten degrees or so, a silhouette of Japanese ships was shown, and was moveable. The instructor could only take so much of my banter, as I was in a "funny" mood that day. He said he was saving me for last. With all the others, he only partially dimmed the lighting. With me, he totally darkened the room. Despite that, I nailed every move, and called every silhouette perfectly. I was elected to stay after "school" and wondered what my punishment would be.

First he ran me though a few more tests, again in total darkness. He was so amazed, he called in his superiors, who also were amazed. After the brass left, he went into hysterics, telling me how perfect my vision is, and that he never ran into anyone like me in all his years doing these tests. He almost died when I told him my secret. Anyone could do what I did. First, I memorized the silhouettes for identification, and next I timed the squeaks in his chains that moved the ship's location on the stage. He became a good friend of mine after that.

    Mr. Bob Hope and his group were getting ready to do their weekly radio show from our Naval Base. His was to follow our regular Navy program. The Navy program was very entertaining, with the highlight being a man who claimed he would put us all into a deep sleep. He did say, however, that he couldn't if an individual didn't believe in hypnotism. I was a non-believer, so I stayed awake. It was very funny, seeing most of my buddies succumb to the ritual. It was explained to us that no person could be hypnotized against his or her will. Having put the majority to sleep, he went down into the audience, and touched four sailors and an Ensign, and had them go onto the stage. As he began narrating, he excused the Ensign, who did admit to faking it. He had them at an Army-Navy game, cheering loudly as Navy scored and booing as Army scored. He told them the weather had turned unbearably hot, and they took off their blouses. He had them order hotdogs, with one of them having mustard accidentally spilled onto his pants.
    One of those on stage was a good buddy of mine. He rarely said two words without swearing, and he let loose with some of them with the mustard incident. Another was chosen to baby sit the Admiral's little girl and had to change her diaper. It was amazing to see him go through the motions. He even pricked himself with the imaginary pin. I can't put in words how funny that program was. The finale was his post-hypnotic suggestion. He had some

newspapers sitting on the apron of the stage. He then touched my buddy and said, "Ninety seconds after you awake, you will take the papers and run up and down the aisle yelling, "EXTRA, EXTRA, HITLER IS DEAD." As he awakened the audience and the ones on stage, we all were checking our watches. In the meantime, those on stage wondered why their blouses were off. Sure enough, after exactly ninety seconds, the paperboy did his stuff.

Now for Mr. Hope. His emcee took sick, and he needed someone to do some introductions for his show. Nothing hard, but to my surprise, my buddies "volunteered" my services. To say I was nervous would be putting it mildly. He was my idol among the comedians of this day and age. This happened in the year 1943. To ease my nervousness, he told me not to start with anything regarding his ski nose, because everybody did. He gave me a one-liner to use, which went over quite big.

I was given a script to follow as to introducing his cast, and then it was his turn to be introduced. He started right out by referring to his ski nose, and then asked me, "What happened to your nose?" Visibly shaken, I used Bob Hope's suggestion and said, "I was washing my hair in toilet water and the seat fell." I'm glad they didn't need me for any more intros, but that joke really turned on the audience. I have used it ever since to lighten up the crowd. It never fails to loosen up any gathering, especially with strangers in the grouping. Mr. Hope was loved by all servicemen for bringing his shows to them no matter where they were. His cast, to name a few as I recall - Jerry Colona, Patty Thomas, Dorothy Lamour - also contributed their services for all servicemen.

We did a retake of this one-liner in Hawaii, sometime in early 1945. The Services utilized the talents of many entertainers. I recall Perry Como came to us in Hawaii, in his early singing career. There were many more, I'm sure, but old age setting in makes it hard for me to remember. I thought of myself as a comedian more than once. Why is it that when a person has a microphone in his hand, he or she thinks it is expected of them to tell a joke, or many jokes? This is even true at funerals nowadays, where it is becoming customary to have loved ones come up with funny episodes involving the dearly departed.

The submariner is a proud member of the "SILENT SERVICE." Why silent? Because once clear of the harbor, radio silence is essential in order not to give away their position. Early in the war, it took a full week or two (or more) traveling submerged most days to get to its assigned stations. As the war progressed in our favor, we could get there faster, running on the surface, at about three times the submerged speed.

To a degree, it became boring, four hours on duty and eight hours off. Every man had a place to be at "battle stations," and activity stopped completely as far as moving around was concerned. If the dive signal was given while on the surface, those on lookout duty and those on the operations deck (usually two officers and a quartermaster) had to move fast, for at the initial dive sound on the Klaxon, the sub is already nose down taking on ballast water in the dive tanks. We are talking in terms of seconds here, with the last man down the conning tower hatch sidling to one side on the ladder and hanging onto the lanyard while the next-to-last man seals the hatch. Sometimes some water comes in, too, if someone was slow clearing the deck. Lookouts had to jump down about ten feet, and usually were the first ones down the hatch. Many practice dives had to be done to make sure nobody was left topside. Nobody??? Not true. Sam Remington, on the first test dive after leaving Vallejo, California, had his binoculars tied up somehow, and luckily he was within earshot of the communication intercom. This happened on his first trip out to sea. I recently found out that this also happened to Leland Flinn, Quartermaster, 99 years old as of this writing. Sam wasn't in as dire straits as Leland, though. Somehow they reversed the dive procedure fast for Sam, but Leland had climbed up onto the periscope shears, figuring sure he was going to have to go swimming. It takes all 88 men to make a perfect dive, working in unison.

Off duty, there was the eternal coffee pot with fresh baked bread available, card games, books to read, repetitious movies to view, and a couple hours of sleep. You didn't know one day from another, one month from another, nor morning or night. All the training in the world could not prepare one for depth charge attacks. Children today think the world ends at our coasts. They have no idea of the vastness of the ocean. While the Pacific usually is calm and placid, I weathered a few storms with waves of fifty feet or more. The waves are measured from the apex to the trough. We could eliminate the discomfort by submerging, but it was most important to keep the batteries charged up in case of encountering the enemy at a moment's notice.

THE SILVERSIDES

The submarine USS Silversides, SS 236, is moored in Muskegon, Michigan, hopefully forever, thanks to Mr. Bob Morin, a most dedicated Silversides backer. Almost single-handedly he has given Silversides what she deserves, and she does deserve the best. She is a survivor. She is the most successful and most decorated submarine of World War II, and the only one of its kind capable of running its engines.

They have an overnight program for Boy Scouts and Girl Scouts that teaches them quite a bit of the history of World War II. As I write this, Mr. Morin has engineered the building of a 16,000 square foot museum which will house many artifacts and educational items, including films.

On shore, by law, the propellers stand, along with World War II torpedoes, and the sail from the submarine drum which was built alongside the Silversides at Vallejo, California. When the museum is completed, Silversides will be the center of attraction. No doubt about it. What most people do not know is that the Submarine service was totally a volunteer division of the Navy. One of four perished. Pray for them, please.

When the Silversides came to Chicago in 1949, or earlier, it was sent there to be a training vessel. Finally the Navy was going to dispose of it and have it cut up into razor blades, and our group found out about it and we decided to start an affiliation. We put ads in the paper and what-not, to save it. Well, Dick Freitag, who was on a different submarine, decided to do something about it. His wife gave him fifty dollars and a businessman bought his airline ticket back and forth, so he went to the Pentagon to talk to the Admiral in charge. The Admiral asked him some questions, like how much money do you have, and Dick lied, giving him an astronomical figure; how many people do you have, and Dick lied again. So the Admiral was kind of leery and said, "Are you sure you can handle this?" Just then the Admiral's secretary came in. She had some papers for the Admiral to sign because it was closing time, and she looked at Dick and mentioned him by name, Dick Freitag, and the Admiral said, "How do you know him?" She said, "Well, he gave tours when he was in charge of the captured World War II German submarine, U-505 in Chicago at the Museum of Science and Industry. He gave tours to Boy Scouts and my son was one and he spent an hour extra answering my son's questions." And the Admiral says, "Okay, you got it." Dick was so happy, he went and had a couple martinis, then he found out he didn't have enough money for the hotel, so he had to call his wife and tell her he was coming in on the red eye special, and that was the end of that. But we did have the submarine under our control. There had been factions in Chicago who tried to wrest it away from us, people who were using the Silversides as their own private weekend getaway.

I went to Norfolk, Virginia, for the dedication of the new SILVERSIDES (nuclear) submarine. This was at a time when our group was at odds with the then-mayor of Chicago, Harold Washington. While our group, the Great Lakes Maritime Museum, were paying the City of Chicago one dollar a year for forty years for docking space at Navy Pier, suddenly, arbitrarily, he wanted us to pay over $50,000 a year.

In Norfolk, Mayor Washington was to be the main speaker. Afterwards, he was talking with a group of reporters when I went up to shake his hand, saying, "I'm not letting go until you give me an appointment." His secretary was nearby, and was told to give me an appointment. He did, for the next Friday at 4:30 p.m. I thought to myself, yeah, sure, I can picture the Mayor staying late in his office on a Friday night.

The meeting went well, however; we parted as friends, the $53,000 was nullified, and we were free to move. The whole fracas was that he wanted our mooring space at Navy Pier for a friend of his. By moving to Muskegon, which move was in the works, we would be solving two problems. I came to Muskegon for a meeting regarding the submarine Silversides. Kay (my current wife) was in attendance, and made some very wise remarks regarding the potential move of the sub to Muskegon. I was quite impressed by her comments, was introduced to her, and I was smitten. I still am to this day. Love at first sight. At that meeting, I was introduced to her by my good friend Dick Freitag. Dick served in World War II on the submarine Blueback. He had a son, also named Dick, who retired from the Navy as a Command Master Chief. Dick put heart and soul into working for the preserving of the Silversides for posterity. Having passed away in 2005, he missed seeing the progress of the Great Lakes Maritime Museum. He would be most proud to see the fruits of his labor with the building of an actual museum right next to the submarine. Every Memorial Day Sunday, we hold a tolling of the boats (for the 52 lost in World War II) where a boat name is called, number of personnel lost is announced, and a rose is thrown into the water in memoriam. Silversides is the only World War II sub capable of firing up its engines. This is done for the many sub vets in attendance.

Because of a treaty with Canada, no military submarines are allowed on the Great Lakes. Needing an ocean-going tugboat to pull us across Lake Michigan from Chicago to Muskegon, we really lucked out. Andre's, the towing company, charged us $1.06 for the move across the lake. I didn't breathe safely until we cleared the Chicago harbor, fearing something would still go wrong. It took twelve hours, and a crowd of over 4,000 were patiently waiting for us in Muskegon. Cars were lined up with their headlights illuminating the channel brightly, a most edifying sight. This was far past midnight, and a reception far greater than anyone imagined.

Tourism is doing quite well in Muskegon, and bookings for the overnight program (where Scout groups, etc., can stay aboard the boat overnight) has no openings except far down the road. Our new museum opened in July, 2008. It is a classy structure and a big plus for Muskegon.

SOME BASEBALL TALK

In the world of sports, baseball was my everything. I can recall playing from morning till dark many days, which is why I did quite well without any outside help.

My "official" baseball career started while still in the Navy, where I played ball on one of their teams. My contract with the Yankees had me playing in Joplin, Missouri, at the start of the spring season in 1947. After a short time I was "demoted" to Fond Du Lac, Wisconsin, where I played through September 4, the end of that season. I was married in December of 1947. I start spring training in Branson, Missouri, in 1948, and quit soon thereafter, as explained elsewhere in this section.

Minor league budgets being what they were, coaching had to be shared by everyone. One day at Fond Du Lac, Wisconsin, I hit a long drive past the center fielder and figured I could make it a home run. A new pitcher just signed at tryout day was coaching at third and waved me to go in as I ran past. He cupped his hands over his mouth, saying "Go on in," then adding, "but I don't think you'll make it." I started laughing, fell to the ground and crawled the last ten feet or so, but I made it. This same pitcher, suiting up his first day with the team, stood in the center of the locker room and asked, "Did anyone bring two right shoes? I brought two left ones." He was serious, too. I wonder if Neil Lettau would remember that? I was the granddad on the team, so he might still be alive and kicking.

Just prior to being sent to Fund Du Lac, my last time at bat for Joplin, I was given the squeeze bunt sign with our fastest runner at third in a close game. Somehow, the opposing pitcher, a former major leaguer, caught the sign also, and threw right at my head. I managed to jump up and backwards to lay down a perfect bunt. He scored and we won the game. I was not in good spirits the next day when informed I was being sent to Fond Du Lac and a player batting less than I was staying on there at Joplin. What irked me most was the sports headline that said "GILMORE STEALS HOME." This was the start of my learning about baseball politics. This was 1947, my first full year. Combining all my at-bats, including spring training of 1948, I averaged .341. I defy anyone reading my scrapbook to tell me I wouldn't have made it to the top. Of course, being Yankee property did make a difference.

Did I really quit? My long cattle car trip home from Branson, Missouri, gave me a lot of time to think. Professional baseball was my dream. There was never ever any doubt in my mind that I would some day play for the White Sox. Here I am, pushing twenty-three years of age. What are my assets? A .341 batting average, I'm fast afoot, a rifle arm. Reading my scrapbook, nobody could tell me I couldn't go to the top. I set up appointments with both the White Sox and the Cubs.

I went to Wrigley Field first. They treated me well; no money was discussed. I related my needs to take my then-pregnant wife with me to wherever they would want me to go. That ended the discussion, except for one thing. The general manager told me "We don't have any luck with Chicago-born players." That was a cop-out, for Phil Cavaretta was in his nineteenth year with the Cubs.

The very next day, I auditioned with the White Sox. I spent the whole night with Red Ormsby, a former umpire. He was the Sox' Illinois and Wisconsin head scout. We rehashed our all-night discussion at Wisconsin Rapids the previous year. He told me then that the Sox were interested in me, that they tried to buy my contract, but the Yankees wouldn't sell. Again, I brought up the subject of money to take my wife along. After all these years, I still hear the voice of John Duncan Rigney coming from the next room saying, "We don't give bonuses." The following Sunday's sports page headline read, "WHITE SOX GIVE 75 G'S FOR BAUMER." The man never played a single game for them to my recollection.

That was my final effort at professional baseball. With tears in my eyes I made my decision to quit dreaming, even though my scrapbook tells me I could have made it big. I rode the streetcars home, a very disillusioned young man. Still a Sox fan, despite their turndown, I will always back them.

On my Mom's deathbed, as we reminisced, she told me that she felt today's players were grossly overpaid. Of course I agreed with her, telling her she had me 40 years too soon. "Would you want me to have you when I was 55 years old?" she asked, to which I jokingly replied, "That would be your problem." Her mind was clear, despite her years. Although she was blind, she kept her TV on and listened to the telecasts. Jokingly I told her that I clearly remembered the day I was born. Her sharp response was, "So do I, Son. So do I." When I told her she needn't use so strong a tone of voice, she said that I was a 25-and-a-half-hour labor child. I then added, "No wonder you didn't have any more boys." She certainly deserved more than I gave her. My first day in first grade, I wet myself and went home. Mom was washing clothes, and when I told her, "Sister sent me home," she took me right back to school. I guess I was a problem for her even after her 25-hour ordeal with me.

MY BELOVED BASEBALL GLOVE

Two pieces of black leather held together mostly by imagination. I cherished that glove, using it all through my career. Never once did I consider buying a new one. In Hawaii, I stationed myself in left field, shagging balls barehanded since nobody was out there. There was an old-timer sitting in the shade, who introduced himself as Schoolboy Rowe. We talked baseball for a while. He then gave me his glove, saying he wouldn't be needing it anymore. It was a relic, but to me, it was a million dollar glove. I must have put on quite a show, because pretty soon several more players joined with the old-timer watching me. There was a set of brothers by the name of Meyers. One was named Don, but the other's name escapes me. I wrote to the White Sox about these brothers, thinking they might consider signing them. The Sox did respond, and thanked me, but the boys already were signed by another club, making it illegal for the Sox to approach them.

I spent many afternoons talking to major league players. I couldn't get enough of them. The Navy housed them on a barge, right next to the ball field. Their only job was to play games to entertain servicemen. Jonny Mize was a joy to talk to. I couldn't even get my hands around his bat handle. Others, to name a few, all wiling to shoot the breeze: Lucadello, Pellagrini, Joe Grace, etc. I wish I could recall the names of the others on service teams playing there in Hawaii. Hickam Field had a man who hit five home runs in a game. Our sub base had a Kenny Sears who hit four home runs in two separate games.

The barges these players slept on were of wood construction, with no windows or doors. The men showered on shore, but these barges afforded great sleeping, being right on the water. I admired them all. No doubt the word should be ENVY, rather than ADMIRED.

Digressing to Fond Du Lac. One day, later afternoon, really, heading to Green Bay for a night game, there seemed to be a black cloud covering the highway. I was told that this was a yearly infestation of a bug dubbed the GREEN BAY FLY. It had a short lifespan, but was so big in body that it was a menace on the highways. They hovered over the highway, basking in the heat of the highway. As if that were not enough, they swarmed at the lights that lit the field of play, and actually caused postponement of the game.

The fairgrounds park was a very legitimate-sized field. Playing center field, I always chatted with the policeman who parked his always shined-up vehicle just over the fence. One night, jokingly, I told him he had best move it, for I felt a home run due. As luck would have it, I did hit one, but missed his car. He said I missed it by a foot, and in the future he was parking it more out of the way for safety's sake.

Another Fond Du Lac memory that is sort of bizarre: The local men's clothing store ran a contest. Their front windows were full of neckties, part of a two-week contest. Guess how many ties and win $100.00 worth of clothing. I forget what my guess was, but I won, missing the exact total by just a few.

There was to be a day in honor of our playing manager, Jim Adlam. Team manager Ernie Wenzlaf owned a music store, where our team gear was stored. I was asked to come up with something because the person in charge had a five-minute gap in his program. Three of us were at Wenzlaf's, whose basement was full of instruments of all kinds. I played the accordion, but the other two couldn't play the radio. With Wenzlaf's son, a top musician, we pulled it off in grand fashion. We deadened the mike at home plate, had the true musicians play for real, and we walked off halfway through a song. Of course, when I asked the crowd what we should play, I heard dozens of their favorites being requested. Our opponents of the night weren't thirty feet away, and they thought we were actually playing, as did the many people the following day in town, who were congratulating me for our musical ability.

Jim was well-liked by the home town fans.

Attendance was about 4,500…

My biggest thrill in sports? After quitting baseball, 16-inch softball kept me going. After the war, South Chicago was the capital of the softball world. Sixteen inch softball, slow pitching was the craze. Every block had a tavern, and every tavern sponsored a team. One of my best friends talked me into joining the team that he managed. George Baranowski was a soft-spoken guy, managing a team that most people didn't like. I joined, and soon learned that what once was considered a sore-headed attitude was strictly a will to win. We really had a great team, one that never gave up.

My greatest thrill? We entered a tournament that started at 7:00 a.m., and if you hadn't lost a game, the championship game began around 7:00 p.m. That's five games in one day. On this day, we were in the last inning, one run ahead with the league's fastest runner on third base. I was in right field, with the opposing team's heavy left-handed hitter up at bat. As expected, he skyed one towards me, and I laid back to take it on a dead run. After catching the ball, I threw a perfect strike right to our manager who was catching. As George caught the ball at ground level, the runner slid into the ball, and we won the game. I know my Uncle John Rybicki was there, but everything else is a blur.

George kept all the scorebooks and may still have them. I would like to see them again. Memories are forever.

WESTERN UNION

NC292 19=NBN NEWYORK NY 28 200P
Gerald F. Bocian 8450 Saginaw Ave. Chgo=
Your telegram of acceptance received. Ward Lambert our representative will call at your home with contract in a few days. Paul Krichell

NATIONAL ASSOCIATION OF PROFESSIONAL BASEBALL LEAGUES OFFICIAL DISPOSITION OF PLAYERS CONTRACT & SERVICES.

To: Gerald Bocian
You are hereby official notified your contract is outright assigned to Fond Du Lac of the Wisconsin State League.
May 19, 1947
From: Joplin Baseball Club
Charles Griffin, Bus. Mgr.

OFFICIAL NOTICE OF DISPOSITION OF PLAYERS CONTRACT AND SERVICES

To: Gerald Bocian
Jan. 28, 1948
Conditionally resigned to Grand Forks of the Northern League.
Fond Du Lac Baseball Club,

"Chiefs" | **THE GRAND FORKS BASEBALL CLUB**
Member of Northern League

March 20, 1948

Grand Forks, North Dakota

Gerald Booian
8450 Saginaw
Chicago, Illinois

Dear Sir:

You are hereby requested to report to the Brown Hotel in Des Moines, Iowa the afternoon of April 2nd.

We have made room reservations for you at the above mentioned hotel and you may use this letter as identification.

Plan on staying there over night and leave for spring training with our group early the morning of April 3rd. Manager Hinkle or myself will arrive at the Brown Hotel with a group of players about 4:00P.M. April 2nd.

If for any reason you are not going to report at the above mentioned place, please notify this office at once.

Yours very truly,

GRAND FORKS BASEBALL CLUB

J. C. Holte, President

JCH/mh

OFFICIAL NOTICE OF DISPOSITION OF PLAYERS CONTRACT & SERVICES

National Association of Professional Baseball Leagues
To: Gerald Bocian
May 4, 1948
You are released outright and unconditionally
Wis. State League, Fond Du Lac, General Mgr.
E. Wenzlaff

FAMILY MATTERS

Our Busia (my grandmother) had to be quite some gal. She stood a towering five feet tall (maybe) and brought at least thirteen children into this world. These were with Grandpa Koch. Grandpa Koch was in the Russian army, and went AWOL to precede Busia's arrival in the United States. Busia came with Mom (Berenice) and a dying boy, name unknown, in 1908. This dying boy, if DOA, would cause them to be returned to Poland. Fortunately, a doctor assisted and kept the child alive until they disembarked. At Grandpa Koch's funeral, I seem to recall Busia saying this was her second trip to Holy Cross Cemetery. Her first was to bury the unnamed little boy.

How did she raise this family? She had a three-flat on Burley Avenue, about three blocks from the steel mills. She took in Polish boarders, got them jobs, and, when they had a few bucks, married them off, sent them out on their own, and brought in more boarders. Then came Grandpa Kaminski. No more children but a bit of a distinction. I have told this to many people, and nobody yet has said they know of a similar situation. Busia had two silver weddings with two different men. Her boys were Barney, Joe, Henry, Matt, Sylvester, Frank, Martin, Stanley; all the boys are gone. The girls were Mom (Berenice), Jennie, Vera, Marcy, and Xaverie. Mom passed away at 98, Jennie just short of a hundred.

In the Frank Bocian family, my family, first there is my oldest sister, Dolores. Dee has eight children. As is usually the case, at first the children settle nearby, but eventually move away, sometimes far away. Ellen is a nurse. Joyce is a business owner in Munster, Indiana; her husband Rick started on a shoestring and all his hard work and perseverance has paid off handsomely. Debbie teaches piano in Vienna, Austria; her husband Dan is also a teacher. They have taught overseas for over thirty years.

Joe and Mike are in sales. Gail is also a piano teacher. Tom works for a state tax department. Tracey is a chemist in the Carolinas. They all made it home for their Mom's 85th birthday party in 2008, including Debbie from Austria. Dee and her husband, Joe, had a tavern business for years, with their whole family participating in the work. Joe, Sr., (Dee's father-in-law) was a calm, cool and collected guy. He sponsored some of the best softball teams in the area.

Joe, Jr., sponsored my bowling team. We, as a team, didn't drink while bowling, but we would gather at the tavern afterwards. When we had our summer cottage in the Indiana Dunes, the Lapotas had one nearby. We had swing sets galore, so when Dee's kids and mine gathered, you couldn't tell them apart; they were all sun-bleached blondes. Some days Joe., Jr., brought his guns and we had target practice against a backdrop of the sandy dunes. Very safe.

Dolores always had a smile as a trademark. She is a positive person, much like Babe, as we affectionately called Bernadine. Babe, however, lost her perpetual smile when her doctor told her she only had three months to live. She turned into a recluse for those first three months but lived for over two years more. At finding out the doctor's three months was a bad guess at best, she lightened up considerably but had no good words for her doctor.

Babe chose the single life. She did over thirty years' service in our State Department, as secretary to ambassadors in French-speaking countries, such as French Indo-China (now Viet Nam), African nations like Chad, the Cameroons, Madagascar, then to Haiti, to Europe at The Hague, Brussels and Paris, and to Montreal, Canada. Some of her stints were duplicate assignments; some, like Paris, were three-timers. In visiting her in Paris, we found out how she wouldn't back down from anyone. When we walked in, she was bawling out the Ambassador for not lowering the toilet seat. After all, she said, the girls outnumbered him two to one. She had an apartment near the Louvre, and she walked to work at the Embassy, being a few minutes late every morning. The reason? She was addicted to watching Casper, The Friendly Ghost. We sat in the Ambassador's box at the Follies. Hearing her rave about how large the stage was, I burst her bubble when I told her about the stages in Las Vegas. On her next leave, we took her to Vegas and proved it to her. She didn't sleep for three days while there. The non-classified info she used to send me would curl your hair. The pettiness of our elected officials was beyond belief. Since she was the top protocol person in the department, she was called to Canada for some meetings in Montreal and Ottawa. It was pretty obvious she loved her work.

Coming home after retiring, she really out-did herself. The job she took upon herself was most compassionate, that of taking care of Mom, full time. Mom was more than a handful. Besides being diabetic, blind, hard of hearing, with very sore knees, and no doubt grouchy most of the time, with all that, Babe endured. It was not easy at first, for they were at each other's throats. However, Babe showed infinite wisdom by giving in at the right time, thereby making life bearable for the two of them. Mom was pushing 98 when she passed. We had great conversations when she was in her last days. She was very alert to the end. I talked to her about the progress that occurred in this (the 20th century. She lamented about several things, mainly about her Christmas parties being abruptly short-lived because of her not-so-famous daughter-in-law. Those parties meant so much to her and the guilty party heaped the greatest insult possible by having the nerve to come to the hospital where Mom was dying, and saying to Babe, "When she awakes, tell her I forgive her." I don't know how Babe kept her composure. I suppose I am at fault in regards to the divorce. I was ostracized by the entire family because I never let on how miserable my marriage was. When I made up my mind to cut it off and got the children together to tell them of my decision, they all said the same thing: "We don't know how you lasted this long, Dad." All my worries about how it would affect Mom were wasted. She said, "You should have left her long ago."

Colette is our world traveler and tourist guide personified. If ever championship rings are given for that category, she would win hands down. With two beautiful daughters, one dynamic, handsome son, and about ten grandchildren, she has been through it all: from farming, to several businesses that weren't so hot, to the present monitoring of several businesses that span half the world, she does it all. In addition to her work, she still qualifies for the tourism medal of honor. When she lived in Florida, almost daily she would be showing friends through Disney World, then taking them to the airport just in time for a new group to be de-planing. Disney should have hired her, or at least given her some commissions. Now they (she and her son Bill) are diversified to the extent that they spend more time in the air than they do on the ground. With businesses in Hawaii, New Jersey, California, and lately New Zealand, it is no wonder that Colette has her hands full. I recall when they lived in the Tampa region, young Bill would go shark hunting in nothing more than a rowboat. Not too long ago, it was the shark hunting Bill. Being an avid surfer, he had a shark bite a chunk off his surfboard. That would be enough for me to get out of the water.

Bill is the ultimate entrepreneur. He was studying at the University of Hawaii when he started making so much money he decided to quit school and devote his time to making money. At that time, Colette and her husband Lloyd Buis had a sun tan lotion business called HAV A TAN. Young Bill sold this lotion to the hotel swimming pool guards and wherever needed. Eventually, he found better sources of making big money. I seem to recall a long time back that he tackled a job nobody else would. That job was washing the porthole windows on the cruise ships. He truly is a hustler, as is Colette.

Alice was a total stranger to me when I returned from the Navy. Her letters to me were precious. She was a baby when I left, and about four or five when I returned. "Part a me" was my favorite part of her letters, meaning "Pardon me"! Alice has a family of three boys and a girl. Jonathan is a doctor; Brian is married and lives and works in Hawaii alongside Bill and Colette; the other boy, Kevin, had aspired to be a boxer, but gave that up. Husband Bob was in Chicago politics and is now retired. Daughter Sandra Lee has three children and lives in Michigan. The Stakes have a summer cottage about five miles from where our home on Magician Lake was. It was a community effort to build, as Grandma and Grandpa Bocian pitched in with the rest. They have enjoyed weekends there, swimming and fishing, for over thirty years. Their property borders on two small lakes, Gear and Round Lakes. I read somewhere that there are 54 lakes named "Round Lake" in the State of Michigan. There is a great sense of being in the deep woods, as their cottage is three to four hundred feet off the road. It is a winding road that enhances the beauty of entering their property.

I consider myself FOUR SISTERS WEALTHY.

The last of this Bocian clan is yours truly (I was second-born), and there is enough said about me in all these pages.

We especially welcomed the snow come the Christmas holidays. I started a trend of throwing snowballs onto the parish hall roof.

The hall was approximately fifty feet away, and forty feet high. Of course when I started that, it became a ritual. I was the only one that could reach the roof. As Dee's boys and my sons started growing up, they threw snowballs closer and closer to the roof, until one day they made it. A classic end to this ritual was a comment by Garry. I don't recall at what age he said it, but it was really funny. His comment? "Boy, there must be a lot of snowballs on that roof after all these years."

The hall was built with a pattern of protruding brickwork, with some bricks protruding one inch. We were too young to know better, but some of our little gang did a very stupid thing: climbing up the face of the hall, hanging precariously by fingertips. Should they fall, there would be nothing but cement to fall on. Besides that, every twelve feet or so there was a cement protrusion that the climber had to muscle over. I shudder just thinking about it. Our parish janitor, also named Jerry, would faint had he seen these climbers. He would let me go up on the roof the safe way, where the belfry was. He lived one block away from us and walked in front of our house six times a day; ringing the bells for noon and other times became such a routine that we could tell the time of day by when he passed by.

Jerry was a very amiable guy. He never failed to greet people as he walked, and everyone knew him. We kids thought ringing the bells would make that job very well worth it, though we never knew what salary he commanded. I know this, his was a seven days a week job, and was on call always.

My intro to being a musician. Dolores did a lot of work for our pastor, who so appreciated her that he gave her a piano. It was an old piano which he had tuned up before having it delivered to our home. I was only about six or seven at the time, and this instrument really caught my fancy. I had Dolores mark the keys for me, and started teaching myself. Of course, I had her to fall back on for any questions that arose. I was doing quite well when the "ham" in me rose to the top. I don't know what prompted this action, but I sat myself under the keyboard and, reaching my right hand up, began playing simple melodies. This really hit a responsive chord with Dad. He insisted that I show all guests my antics. Of course, being the shy guy that I was, he didn't have to ask me twice. Soon, I graduated back to normalcy, and liked playing so much that I asked Mom if I could take lessons from the nuns. Sister Eleutheria was my teacher (later re-named Sister Lou Marie). I really felt a sense of accomplishment as I progressed from simple songs to more classical tunes.

After marriage, I bought a spinet organ, and later on, a Hammond Concorde, which was a beautiful instrument. As long as we had large homes, it moved from home to home with us. Soon after my divorce, though, finding room for it was a problem. Janine had it for several years, but then ran out of space too. It ended up with Babe for many years. With Mom there, I was always called upon for her favorite songs to sing. In fact, Babe used to call in her neighbors for a sing-along. Eventually, after her passing, some charitable organization was called to pick it up. No doubt it is being used wisely now, and some good is to come of it. I hate to think of it sitting someplace deteriorating. It certainly left me with many happy memories. I do have another spinet to entertain myself and Kay, but Parkinson's is taking its toll. God bless the Felicians.

A funny story that cannot be forgotten: Grandpa Bocian was asked to baby sit, which he did. I think TV sit would be more appropriate. While he had his eyes glued to the football game, the little ones were in the basement. Somehow, they opened up a new can of paint, put their feet into the can, and then proceeded to make tracks all over the basement. Grandpa said, "They are fine, they are quiet in the basement." I don't recall him getting that job again.

Before mentioning my family, and before I forget, I have another Dad story. Dad made home brewed root beer, positively the best I ever tasted. One night I asked for a second bottle after dinner, and the response was a definite NO. I decided that somehow I would satisfy my thirst for the evening. I waited until the girls were in bed and my folks were in the front room. My bedroom was just off the kitchen pantry, so I could watch the folks and sneak into the pantry. I thought I was really clever, reaching behind me and grabbing a bottle and taking a long cool drink. Guess what? It was a bottle of VINEGAR. Mom and Dad laughed and I'm sure the neighbors heard me yelling, too. This never happened again, so I must have learned my lesson.

Family? Boy do we ever have a family. I tried to get a picture of the entire family while we were having a get-together at Alice's summer cottage. I set my camera on the roof of my car, set for wide angle, with a timing device so that I could get into the picture too. I wish I had a Polaroid then, because by the time I had the film developed, I found out I had cut off about eight persons on one side of the picture. Forty-nine was my actual count of those who did make it into the photo. See what Busia started? I was asked how she managed raising thirteen children. If you think about it, thirteen children with her first husband in twenty-five years is quite a feat in itself. She had a small house, so come Christmastime, we had to come in platoons. It didn't matter how many came, or when; she had enough food for an army. Mom had a much larger home, and really looked forward to her Christmas parties.

My family? It is hard to imagine my children growing up in such an unhappy marriage. I sometimes feel fate dealt Lucille a bad hand, in that she had constant migraine headaches due to a chemical imbalance. That caused me to file for divorce (after 44 years) to save my own sanity. How well the children survived is a tribute to their ability to withstand the sudden changes in their mother's attitude. I will be forever grateful for having such a wonderful group. When I introduced them to Kay, upon my decision to file, they all said, "We didn't think you would last this long, Dad."

First came Christine in 1949, a good student (they all were), and, being the oldest of the children, the one who had it the toughest growing up. Naturally, she would get the babysitting job whenever needed. She won three of six awards, as I recall, in her business class. In an almost-forgotten brave move, she saved us from what could have been an inferno. Halloween brought out the artist in me, as I cut out a pumpkin, put in a lit candle, then placed it in the front window. Paul was playing with some paper thing and dropped it into the pumpkin. Chris came running into the kitchen, bravely holding the pumpkin upright. We had the carpeting cleaned that day, and had she dropped that flaming pumpkin, the chemicals used by the carpet cleaners would certainly have started the house on fire. She married Marvin, a lawyer, and they have a beautiful daughter, Alexandra. Marvin is well-versed in all subject matters, and quite a historian. Alex was a ranking gymnast in Illinois during her high school years. She has studied in Germany and hopes to end up living and working there after finishing university. Chris and Marv brought home a German dachshund that tires me out just from watching it play "soccer". Of course, at my age, it doesn't take much to tire me out. They live in Indian Head Park, Illinois.

Paul, born in 1951, is now a retired fire captain from the LaGrange Fire Department. He is an absolute genius at anything he tackles. He is a master of the stained glass business, working out of his home in Brookfield, Illinois. Paul built a kidney-shaped koi pond in his back yard. For some of his siblings, and for Kay and me, he built beautiful decks. There seems to be no end to his talents. He has had his bad moments, too. One day when he was maybe eight years old, playing out in front of our home, he was hit with a softball bat, just missing an eye. I rushed him to the hospital for stitches, and he mended well. Exactly one month later, as I was coming home after making a delivery with my station wagon, just about one block from home, I saw this boy lying in a pool of blood. I had carpeting protecting the rear of the wagon, and placed the boy inside. Imagine my surprise when I heard him talk, and found out that it was Paul. This time he caught a rock in the other eye. I again rushed him to Holy Cross Hospital, where the ER nurse (a nun) said, "You again?" I thought they might consider charging me with child abuse. Now that he is a big boy, he has another claim to fame. Paul periodically invites us all to his now-famous snack parties. They go over big as we continuously eat, but don't overeat. We pace ourselves.

LETTER FROM THE THIRD RECRUIT RAINING CENTER

SAN DIEGO, CA 92140
SEPT 27, 1969

Mr. Gerald Bocian
6745 W. Menominee
Palos Hgts., IL 60563

Dear Mr. Bocian:

I am pleased to inform you that your son, Private First Class Paul L. Bocian, 2570757, U.S. Marine Corp., has been chosen to receive a Dress Blue Uniform awarded by the LEATHERNECK Magazine to the outstanding recruit in the platoon. The Commanding Officer, Recruit Training Regiment Marine Corps Recruit Depot, will issue a letter of recognition to your son for his achievement.

In order that you may have a complete understanding of your son's accomplishment it should be noted that he won this coveted award in competition with 75 men, all of whom entered the Marine Corps and progressed through training with him. From that number and on a recommendation of his drill instructors, the Marines in this platoon displaying the highest order of skill and professional knowledge in a wide range of basic military subjects were closely examined. After considering the knowledge, conduct, attitude, military bearing, and leadership potential of all the candidates, your son was judged most worthy to receive the Marine Corps' Dress Blue Uniform. We in the Marine Corps are intensely proud of our dress blue uniform. It is the opinion of those who mostly closely observed Private First Class Bocian that he will wear it with distinction and honor. We are indeed proud to have a young man of such high caliber in our ranks.......D. R. HINES, US Marine Corps, San Diego, CA 92140

Donna next appeared in 1954. She was our attention seeker. We bought a summer cottage at the foot of Lake Michigan, with a pristine white sand beach, with some gravel included. Donna simply didn't like the gravel to hit her knees, so she sidled like a crab, on all fours. I carried her around in a two-gallon bucket. Her biggest attention grabber was the three steps from a landing going downstairs, into the kitchen and back. Whenever we would be in the house, a big THUD told us it was Donna. The bottom three steps were from the room addition at the back of the house. She and friend Mark Dahme are Harley owners, and come up to Michigan for bikers' doings every year. They too have a beautiful home in Bolingbrook. Donna works for an IHC dealer. She worked for us in our trucking business for years, as did all the kids. Donna has two boys, Shaun and Eric. Shaun (and his wife Amy) presented us our first great grandchild this past January 2007, a beautiful boy named Vincent.

Garry arrived in 1956. He is my golfing guru. He eats, drinks and sleeps golf, and rightly so, for he is very good at it. One day I had two foursomes scheduled for a customer outing, when we found ourselves one man short. Garry was at the office, and I called him out to fill out our group. He didn't need any prodding. I placed him in the second group and we were all set. In those days I hit a long drive. Preparing to hit my second shot, a ball came whistling over my head. It was Garry, playing barefoot. I thought I could cure that by buying him shoes, but he only got better and better. I feel proud of his game today and the fact that I played a small role in it. He is a real sportsperson. Right now he is in New Jersey, running a company for his cousin Bill. They manufacture floor scrubbing machinery, and Bill is a genius, having businesses in California, New York, Hawaii, and New Zealand. Garry can adapt to anything. He started working for me licking stamps at age eight. He is proficient at handling 18-wheelers, lift trucks, or any number of pieces of machinery.

Son Neil was next, being born in 1960. Before his life came to a tragic end at 31, he left us with some memories. After leaving the Air Force he obtained his private pilot's license. Aspiring to become an airline pilot, he made contact with every airline at Midway Airport, as well as O'Hare, to no avail. In order to beef up his resume and add many hours to it, he took a job flying for a sky diving club in West Chicago. He said it was boring, but he stuck with it. One day, from the plane directly in front of him, the diving instructor jumped out without his parachute. This so unnerved Neil that he quit.

Another short story on Neil. He came home very dejected one day. He was playing soccer for his high school, Marist, and scored a goal. I tried to congratulate him, until he told me that he scored for the other team by kicking the ball into his own net. He did have a strong leg, kicking the ball the length of the field at times.

Neil was a dreamer, and not being able to enter the Air Force flight school because he didn't have a college degree devastated him. He had aspirations of building himself a home up high in the Rockies. In addition, he had visions of building himself a home in the northeast. I loved to hear him talk about those visions. Of course, all was predicated on an airline pilot's salary. Neil worked for me in the trucking business until joining the Air Force. Like Garry, he handled semis and all of our equipment very well.

Finally, born in 1963, Janine brings up the rear. She is a most compassionate person, teaching severely handicapped children.

She and her husband Tom now have two children of their own, Ian and Sydney. Janine opted to get a foster child about twenty years ago, not specifying race or gender. They sent her a two-year-old Afro-American girl, Tamika, who really gave her a challenge. At the time, Janine was not married and had no children of her own. Tamika could not, and would not ever walk. Being a coke baby, Tamika had two strikes against her already. Janine was also told Tamika would not talk but eventually she had Tamika singing and saying some words. Janine (and eventually Tom) lovingly cared for Tamika as their own. Tamika was really a brilliant child and we all loved her. When Tamika turned about eight, Janine became pregnant, and had to make a decision that saddened us all. With Tamika now in a full body cast, the possibility of losing her baby caused Janine to give Tamika up because of Tamika's added weight. Tom and Janine have a lovely home just south of Joliet, Illinois.

Living in Muskegon, Michigan, two hundred miles away from four of my children, is a hardship and I miss seeing them more often. We are a close family, and I consider myself richly blessed.

BACK TO OLD MEMORIES

Sitting at the dinner table, enjoying a polish sausage dinner one evening, the subject of child molesters was broached. Paul seemed to take a dim view of the importance of the subject. He felt adamant that he could simply run away from such a person. I told him that these persons do not announce who they are. Then I made a big mistake, saying, "Besides, you can't even beat me in a race." After this statement, it was suggested we run the race right after supper. There I was, a slim 250 pounds, challenging this teenager. I was trapped. But I did get in the fact that we run by my rules. Living on a street with a cul-de-sac at one end shortened the run. I pointed out the route we were to take and I was really shaken to see every home had witnesses on their front porches to watch this debacle. Well, I won the race, but I CHEATED. I kept Paul slightly back of my right shoulder so when he started gaining, I moved over in front of him to keep myself in the lead. When it was over, I had to sit for a long time to rest. I tried to console Paul by saying, "How do you feel?" He said, "I feel find, Dad, BUT YOU DON'T." He was right. If I ever was close to a heart attack, that was the time.

I came home to dinner one night to a very sober atmosphere. Lou told Garry to tell me what he had done. Very sheepishly, Garry said he took one of my home run balls and scuffed it up on the street. I had all my home run balls signed with information of the time and place, etc. I told him to take them all, for they are no longer of use to me. Needless to say, this irked his mother no end, for she placed a bigger value on those balls than I did.

In 1957, we bought a summer cottage on the southernmost tip of Lake Michigan. It was a very rustic building, with no running water, no refrigeration, and no electricity. It was a very peaceful setting, surrounded by dunes on all sides, situated about 500 feet from the lakeshore, and on a hill about seventy-five feet above the lake level. We rented the lot from the Bethlehem Steel Company for $125.00 a year, knowing that at any time they could decide to build and we would be expected to move out. Being just an hour's

drive from home, we figured it would be like a vacation every weekend, and well worth the price. It started out as a one-bed cottage (the owner was in his nineties) and, thanks to our two fathers, it soon became a veritable lodge that slept over ten persons. They built (we did help some) an addition to the main building that slept at least eight, and then another building, about 12 by 20 feet with the front end housing a 6-foot tool shed, and a toilet with no running water. My genius Dad decided that we would have running water. Thanks to my father-in-law's (Lou's father) truck to haul in all our materials, he brought in about ten 55-gallon drums. These were tied together in rows of five, stacked high behind the 12 by 20 building, where they caught the rainwater off that building. They were all tied together in sequence. All I had to do in the spring is to put in a plug into the lowest drum, and the rest would naturally fill up depending on the amount of rain. For five years, we always had sufficient water to flush the toilet. We did have the old-fashioned outhouse, which Mr. Sniegowski thought was priceless. He was a gentle soul, a house mover by trade, and easy to get along with. Our parking facility was about 500 feet from the cottage, and between the two fathers, we soon had a walkway made of creosoted planks.

Since we always carried supplies in on our shoulders, this walkway was a godsend. Thanks to Mr. Sniegowski and his truck, and my Dad's getting clearance from his superiors to haul away these planks, things happened.

The added building was going to be just 10 by 10, but Mr. Sniegowski brought two 20 foot beams, since he had them to spare. This added building served also as our boathouse. We had two air-filled "sausages" on which we rolled the boat up and down the hill, to and from the lake. The boat was a 15 foot runabout with a 35 horsepower Mercury outboard. The boathouse was on the lower level of the building, while the upper level had a very large "changing room" (to keep wet sand out of the house) behind the tool shed and toilet.

One Sunday, while we were eating lunch, a small plane came flying in over our heads, landing on the beach. The pilot said he had water in the fuel causing the landing on our beach. Neighbors Stan Wolsic and his wife Angie were our guests that day. When the pilot finished clearing out his fuel lines and felt ready to take off, Stan and I, each at the wingtips, helped him get airborne by pushing him through the soft sand till he got up enough traction. Strangely enough, no crowd gathered, unless they were all having lunch at that time. The ideal thing about this location was that there were only about sixty of us having cottages along this stretch of shoreline.

We did have a catastrophe one Sunday. We were separated from a community called the Ogden Dunes by a waterway called Burns Ditch. That area was just the opposite from ours, in that whereas we were residing in rustic homes, they had spacious and luxurious residences. One weekend, one of their group was entertaining a Boy Scout Troop. The lake was particularly nasty that day, with heavy winds making it dangerous for some activities. One of the scouts was out on an air mattress, and soon drifted far from shore, and drowned. We felt helpless, and prayed, but there was nothing anyone could do. If only their leader would have taken precautions.

After about five years of "heaven" at our little cottage, Bethlehem Steel decided to build a huge steel mill on the property, and we lost our lease. They flattened all the dunes, and their "monstrosity" sits there to this day.

We did a lot of searching for another "cottage". We finally found an ideal location, just 15 miles east of Benton Harbor in the Sister Lakes region of Michigan. We found a lot for sale and decided to build a year-round home on it. Magician Lake was beautiful, about seven miles long, a mile wide. Our lot was on the shallow side, where you could walk out 200 feet and still only be shoulder deep. We put out a pier that extended 80 feet, and had a fleet of a rowboat, catamaran sailboat, and a speedboat; something for everyone. I won two snowmobiles, which made our winter weekend trips more enjoyable.

We purchased the lot next door, put in a sprinkling system, grassed it in, and toward the roadside put in a concrete slab for a basketball court. We didn't have a TV set, nor did we need one with all the activities available. Sitting by the fireplace watching the burning embers was entertaining. If that wasn't enough, having our friends the Rekruciaks over for card games was fun also.

One day we had a tornado come through. Janine and I watched (foolishly, instead of taking cover) as boats were being flipped over. Our sailboat mast dug into our front lawn. Had it not, it would have come right at us through the front windows. We were without electricity for several days. Needless to say, we had food but no way to cook it. All roads were blocked with fallen trees, and we began a search for several of our kids who had gone fishing just before the storm came through. It was scary, for tree branches partly submerged looked like possibly a child's body. Other than our sailboat, our fleet was intact. Our immediate neighbor's pontoon boat was flipped over their dock, upside down on its roof. There was one tragedy. Our lake had two islands. One had a young boy visiting and sleeping in an upstairs bedroom. A huge oak tree fell on the upper bedroom, killing the boy.

SPECIAL TIMES
WITH THE CHILDREN

I can think of a lot of anecdotes that fit this subject. Father-Daughter dances, and Janine's especially stand out in my mind. Why, I don't know, but somehow it does. I must have mangled her feet the way I danced.

Donna, having gone to three high schools, and then, in her first month at St. Joseph's College, in Rensselaer, Indiana, the administration building burned. She called us in tears, so we drove there to view the damage. We already know her aversion to three steps up or down, don't we?

Garry went to St. Joseph's, too, and graduated in three years. He hasn't told me, to this day, the record he set on getting parking tickets at that school. He simply did not believe those "No Parking" signs were meant for Garry Bocian. He sustained himself by working as a truck driver for some granary. Working for me in my trucking business gave him the basics for handling any type of trucks.

Chris and Marvin made the Grand Canyon raft trip special. Marv's birthday (June 17) was celebrated with a special cake made by one of our guides, using only seven pieces of charcoal (more on that trip later). Another Chris story: She was very young at the time and she was told that the statue of the Blessed Virgin was a statue. In trying to repeat it, she said, "Oh, stat me?" We had to laugh.

Most precious time with Paul: October 6, 2007. That's when I fell and ruined my right hip, and re-injured my right knee. I never experienced more pain in my life than I felt from that fall. He had the paramedics and ambulance there in no time at all. I could, in fact, write another book just on my children and our experiences.

Neil was a dreamer. My memories of our discussions on flying were classics. He certainly was responsible for kindling the flying bug in me.

Kay has a wonderful family too. They have accepted me, and are a fun group to be around. Son Rick Homoly, father of three beautiful girls, is a contractor, dealing in cement primarily. Rick has built four or five homes in which they have lived, as with the present one. Debra, his wife, copes very well with all their problems. One of the girls has a health problem requiring all of Debra's talents (nothing she cannot handle). Rick has a dry sense of humor and likes to banter back and forth with me. His youngest, Hailey, is a highly intelligent youngster with a very high IQ. She challenges me all the time. Next in line is Brooklyn, a straight A student. She too is full of humor, which is nice. Autumn, the eldest, is studying to be a nurse while working in restaurants. Most holidays are spent at Rick's, which is what he wishes. He is a family man personified. Rick has seven to ten acres.

Kay's youngest, Cindi, is an animal lover. She has about seven acres, two or three dogs, three geese, a cat, and had a horse until recently. She is a multi-talented person. Cindi can do anything asked of her, and she will do it well. She is searching for her niche in life. Her husband is a serviceman for Comcast. I wish I knew something about electronics, or even mechanics.

Kay's eldest, Christine, is in realty, and doing a great job. She and husband Bernie have two boys, BJ and Chad, both excellent hockey players. We have seen their development since they were toddlers, and know they could make the grade in the game of hockey. Bernie has a sign business, a very successful one, and is originally from Newfoundland, Canada, and a good hockey player in his own right. Both he and Chris are soft-spoken individuals and are business oriented.

Kay's Mom and Dad. I came to Muskegon too late to enjoy much of her Step-Dad. He was a jokester and a very pleasant conversationalist. Sorry to say, most of my time with him was while he was immobilized at home or in hospitals. I fancied myself as a better than average cribbage player, until one day he challenged me to a game. To say he showed me a thing or two would be putting it mildly. Good thing we were not playing for money!
Now, Kay's Mom is a different story. She was a funster, always a step ahead of me. For instance, for a person with macular degeneration, one who supposedly couldn't see well, get this. Here she is, riding in the back seat of our car, when I didn't quite come to a full stop at a stop sign. Within two seconds, she comment, "You can stop twice at the next stop sign." She was a wonder to take along on auto trips, or plane trips. She never complained. She sat in the back seat of our car so quietly that we had to ask if she was awake. Of course, seated in and amongst all our luggage, it would be simple for her to doze off. We had her at Disney World one time, and she thoroughly enjoyed it. She was game for anything we would suggest. We took her to San Diego to visit her grandson, and at the airport, she was stuck in a faulty elevator in her wheelchair. Another trip to Seattle to visit another grandchild, found yours truly falling at a golf course, ending up in the full body brace, and Kay ending up pushing two wheelchairs around airports on the way home. We have had our share of memorable moments. She was precious. I was told that it is unheard of for anyone to take a mother-in-law on vacation. I defy anyone to find a better traveling companion than Ovelia Gilbert. She was a

sweetheart, and I truly miss her. In fact, I was blessed in having three Moms and Dads that anyone would be happy to claim. What have I done to deserve all these blessings?

Just when things are looking good, I find a way to screw it up. October 6, 2007, I went to my son Paul's house to go with him to a retirement party for one of my drivers. The party was nice, but the next day was a real downer. I slipped on a small rug, went crashing to the floor, shattered my right hip, and wrenched my right knee. I was in excruciating pain and let the entire neighborhood know it. Paul, just out of the shower, came down and immediately called 911. In short order, I was on my way to the hospital in LaGrange, Illinois, two hundred miles from home. After a week there, I was moved to Manor Care in Hinsdale, Illinois, for rehab. A couple days after arriving, I developed a 105.5 fever and urinary tract infection and was sent back to LaGrange Memorial Hospital for three or four days, until everything was under control. Then it was back to Manor Care until December 14th, where I underwent rehab twice a day and lost forty pounds along the way. Kay came in to Chicago to see me when I had the fever and infection, and then one other time she came for my grandson Shaun's wedding, which I was also allowed to attend. All that time we were apart, and I was not a happy camper. Sometime in between invasive visits from nurses (like every five minutes), I had contacted a stomach infection and continued problems with the urinary infection. Other than that, everything went well.

Paul drove me home on December 14th. What a homecoming that was. While I was gone, Kay redid my bedroom: new drapes, new paint job; she did an absolutely great job. Of course, I wasn't there to bother her. I am still doing rehab myself, for the knee is very slow in healing, though the hip is fine. My base of my spine is very bad and I go to a pain clinic for shots periodically. Hey, other than that, I'm the picture of health. Without Kay, how would I manage? I have edemic hose she puts on me daily. It is a chore for her, very tight fitting, and rough to put on. She also keeps track of my meds, keeps me in vitamins, and does all the heavy lifting now. I sure feel helpless in my condition. I pray some day I will be of help again.

Kay is my nurse, my secretary, my everything. She has coped with all my health problems, and there have been many to say the least. Several years ago, I had a bout with melanoma, when they cut a four inch by six inch cancerous slice out of my chest. During their handling of that problem, they found I had an erratic heartbeat, and I have been taking Coumadin ever since. I already had one total knee replacement, and now needed another. Then, two cataract removals were urgently necessary. It seems the old saying, "When it rains, it pours", was never truer spoken.

Kay has a Bridal Shop. She is very talented, and when decorating a church or hall she doesn't leave unless everything is in top shape. Part of her hall décor was hanging draped lighting from the ceiling. I did that, but no longer can I climb the ladders, so she isn't selling that facet of her business any more. In fact, she is trying to turn her business around, dealing more in dresses for mothers of the brides. Decorating halls is not too bad, but we have to go back at midnight to take everything down. THAT is the rough part, getting us home at two or three a.m. Once in a while, we would luck out and get an okay to pick up the next day (Sunday), but that was few and far between. Many times, she would book two weddings for the same day, and there were times as many as three. Talk about a fiasco, those were the days.

The wedding business as we knew it is drying up. It's not that people aren't getting married, but it is a fact that people are doing their own decorating. Invariably, they come back and say they wished they had listened to us because of how hectic the day went. Because of Kay's expertise, of course, we get thank you letters for the great job she does. One woman wrote to Kay while on her honeymoon, thanking Kay for the great job she did.

I can now state that loving my children was high on the list of my loves and right up there at the top of the list is my Kay. She is a most remarkable person. I have never met anyone like her. She is most considerate, respectful and loyal to whatever she deals with. The dictionary doesn't have enough suitable worlds to properly describe her attributes. A song was written about her: "Love is Wonderful the Second Time Around."

CHICAGO-MIAMI TERMINALS, INC.

A successful part of my life, a tribute to hard work and resolve, was the starting of my own trucking company. It was named CHICAGO-MIAMI TERMINALS, INC. Since I was working two or three jobs to maintain my family needs, I decided to work for myself rather than make big money for others. I did not take extra jobs to put money in the bank, but rather for definite purposes, like a new car or an addition to the back of our new home. I had a partner who gave all our earnings to the horses. What the horses did with it, I don't know. With that first partner, we had a great young man named Al Tate working for us. He was hard-working, honest and loyal. I broke up with my first partner, and knowing without help I would not last very long, I gave Al Tate 50 percent of my company, much to the chagrin of my wife.

    We were a perfect pair when we got it going; he did the dock work while I did the sales. I traveled ten states here in the Midwest, digging up business, and, eventually, traveled all through Central and South America and the Caribbean. Being away from my family was difficult, but it paid off considerably. Dealing in export commodities only, we started handling the exports for Admiral, Zenith, Motorola, and others.

We had a natural edge over our competitors for we began working with Armellini Express Lines out of Stuart, Florida. They provided us with trailers to load as soon as they emptied (they hauled fresh flowers northbound), and with two men in a truck, second morning delivery to Miami was a shoo-in. We expanded our business gradually, taking on new accounts only if their scope of operation didn't conflict with what we presently had. Service was the name of the game in those days. Today, money talks, discounts abound, and service is just another word in the dictionary. Sometimes, we had worries as to service, when we had an abundance of freight, and no trailers to load. Then we were forced to use rail and pray.

We had some bad situations arise when using the railroads. Their service ethics paled in comparison to ours. Once, they "lost" a loaded trailer for three weeks. We were in a real bind. Our very existence was based on our fast service to Miami. I don't recall how we got out of it but for a company having a policy of NEVER lying to anyone, we must have performed some sort of miracle. I do remember that a railroad man saw the name "Armellini" somewhere on that trailer, and sent it to their home office in Vineland, New Jersey. While we were glad to know where it was finally, we had a lot of people to convince we were merely humans. I think I was on a sales trip at that time, and glad of it. With my first partner now history, Al Tate handled everything in a masterful manner. Al drove semis when only fifteen years old. He had a lot of experience to add to our business.

Some of our regular accounts wanted to know why we couldn't handle their domestic Miami business. Al told them to simply put "for export" on their bill and we would do the rest. We kept a separate file on those shipments. One day, the ICC in Washington, D.C., in answer to a competitor's inquiry, summoned us to a hearing. During the proceedings, the commissioner questioned me whether we could deliver to Miami in two days. We spilled the contents of three file boxes on his desk, saying "We have been doing it for three years." We knew that we could continue that movement until a CEASE AND DESIST order would be rendered to us. After that order we must stop or face loss of operating authority. The commissioner was very impressed, and granted us the ability to continue as we were, so Armellini Express no longer was restricted to export freight only. Their northbound cut fresh flower hauling was exempt anyway, so this ruling was a most welcome decision.

The Armellini family was something special. They were customer-oriented to a fault. Mr. Armellini was known for his suggesting ways for flower growers to increase their income, even though he ended up with less for himself. When I was forty, he asked me if I golfed. I didn't at that time. He told me that you can get more business on the golf course than you can imagine, and he was right. I never became proficient at it, but had fun. Quite often, we had meetings in Miami or Stuart. After meetings, we did golf sometimes, or go to the Jai Alai Fronton.

While I never excelled at golf, I did at betting at jai alai. One night, six of us went, and I was voted in as the one who would place the bets, collect the winnings, etc. We won a few small bets and then hit a trifecta for $3,800.00. When I went to collect, I was asked for my social security number. When I told the cashier I was to split with five others, she simply said she needed their social security numbers or no payout, sorry. It was a long way back to where we were seated, so I told her to put it all on my social security number. She told me, after paying me, to pick up losing tickets off the floor, to the exact amount of the win, which we did. I paid them off and carefully put the losing tickets in my pocket. I had those losers in an envelope on my desk just waiting for the IRS to call. Through two moves of our facility, the losers went with me. Over a year and a half later, two days after I threw away the losing tickets, guess what? The IRS called and I had to pay the taxes, for we were losing our connection with Armellini Express Lines. Of the six of us, I collected just one portion. Just my luck.

While on sales trips, I had a few situations occur. Once, in San Salvador, I asked my Miami counterpart, Eduardo Baccallao, for names of accounts I should call on while there. He didn't respond till the day I was leaving, giving me just one account to see. The company I visited was run by a woman who had a rattan furniture business along with a coffee plantation. She showed me around, took me to a mountain village, where a man was making leather soccer balls. I bought one, giving him ten US dollars, though he asked three. It was interesting. As we were flying out, I saw the airport was ringed with brush fires. It was only after I arrived at Miami that I found out I was looking out the window at the beginning of a siege. Thanks, Eduardo.

VENEZUELA, A CHANGING COUNTRY

Since Venezuela was our strongest ship-to country, it necessitated my making sales trips periodically down there. At one time, I felt very safe and comfortable on my sales trip there, but I know that this would no longer be the case with present Communist control. They used to pattern their politics to ours. They had a rather unique presidential term, six years, and no succeeding yourself, with a mandatory year's hiatus at government expense. This hiatus prevented any diehards from creating a problem for the new regime. Now, under Communist control, it's a different story.

I had to plan my appointments around their siesta times. I only got caught short one time, when I had a lunch appointment (late morning) at the Humboldt-Sheraton on the mountaintop above Caracas. Since I used the tramway to get to my appointments at the seashore, I thought I was right on schedule, but I forgot one thing. I read the schedule of the tramway wrong. I caught the in-between tram, and was hung up at the halfway point on the downside. It didn't turn out too bad, as I had a great view of a bocce ball tournament. I guess this was a ritual for those who handled the tramway. They made me comfortable, so the two-hour siesta went by fast.

I made my sales calls, and spent the rest of the day checking the registers of the ships at anchor in the bay. There were over 100 freighters out there awaiting their turn to unload. This backup was caused by a union squabble. My concern was to find out how long my accounts would be waiting for deliveries.

How much coffee can one drink? A demitasse cup is small, but filled one-third with Espresso and two-third with sugar, makes one feel like they are floating at sea. Every office, at every contact, had an Espresso machine, and it was impolite to turn them down. While at that time, between the sixties and the eighties, I was not dieting, the caloric count must have been huge. Eventually I learned how to politely turn them down when offered. I learned and unlearned conversational Spanish before and after my planned sales trips to Latin America. The old saying, "If you don't use it, you lose it," still holds true. I must admit, however, that my contacts always wanted to try out their limited use of the English language, so it was fun in the long run.

One trip I took a tour and was shown beautiful high rises the government was building for the needy who covered the mountainside with their tin and cardboard huts. It seemed that each had a TV antenna showing. On my next visit, the beautiful high rises were in shambles, and the mountainside was back to where it had been. It seemed the government failed to teach them how to live in a neat apartment.

The people I met were friendly, well-dressed, and always smiling. Gunther Piek, VIASA AIRLNES' sales executive, gave me every consideration and actually gave me one of his best people to take me around faster to my appointments. I sponsored them all to a dinner, and it was kind of funny, really. We were Polish, German, Swiss, French, English, Dutch, Danish and Venezuelan. Thank goodness Gunther handled all translations to perfection.

One evening I attended a baseball game. The ball field was in the heart of town. I saw armed guards all around, and the parking was unbelievable. There were no aisles. People pulled in right behind one another, leaving barely enough room to walk by. I thought to myself, "What if someone needed medical attention?" After the game, I understood the armed guards' need. There were guards every fifty feet at the game, too. Fighting broke out in the stands every fifteen minutes or so, but was quietly handling by the guards. Getting out of the parking lot was quite a challenge.

On one of my trips to Venezuela, I purchased air tickets called "SKY BUY". This was a first-time offer, and certainly worth the price, as it covered unlimited air travel within the country for thirty days. I first used it for a trip to Canaima. It was a jungle setting by a waterfall, looking like Niagara, but only about twenty feet high. It was about twenty miles to the foot of Angel Falls, the world's highest waterfall. Before landing, our pilot flew us close to the falls, which come out of the mountain about fifty feet blow the top. The plane that Jimmy Angel crashed atop this mountain is still there. He walked away and got back to civilization by some miracle.

Back at Canaima, we were the only English-speaking couple until a diamond prospector came up and asked if we would take his diamonds to the States. Of course our answer was no. Then, another English-speaking couple flew in in their own plane, a small single-engine aircraft. When we started conversing, we found that the gent was a CEO from Bethlehem Steel Company, the same firm that we rented the dunes land from. It certainly is a small world.

Due to the remoteness of Canaima, they must fly in two planes, one being for a possible emergency. Shortly before our plane was to leave, the empty plane flew out, just over our heads, it seemed. I would have liked to fly out in that single-engine aircraft. Canaima is about 400 miles south of Caracas. Another Sky Buy trip was to the city of Maracaibo. Included in this trip was a steak dinner, and since the flight is only one hour and ten minutes long, we could take that flight every night. I do not know what one would encounter down there today, and I don't think I would want to find out.

On a sales trip to Puerto Rico, I found myself in the middle of another fiasco. It seems there was a faction who wanted to become another US state, so power was cut off on the entire island. Since I was going to show the Armellini display case, I had to go into the cargo hold of the plane in my new suit to dig out my display case, which measured four feet by five feet by four inches. Thank goodness for cabbies. Shaving by candlelight was no picnic, but the only thing that went right was my luck at the casino. They made certain that their generators were working. It was such a stressful day that I quit gambling and decided to go to bed.

Kay liked it there. Our suite was on ground level, within 50 feet of the beautiful pool and waterfall. I fell asleep and was awakened by Kay who seemed frantic, saying

"Jerry, Jerry, there's a man in the room." I awoke just in time to see some guy wheel around, two drinks in his hands with ice cubes tinkling, not saying a word, but out the door in a hurry. She was also enamored by our visit to the rum factory. The place was ultra clean, and we took a tour of the factory, sampled some rum drinks, and since we missed the last bus, ending up taking a boat across the harbor to the El Moro Castle.

FLYING

Flying, my fondest dream. In the summer of 1942, my good friend Frank Byers spent almost every day on the 79th Street beach, watching the Navy flight trainers do take-offs and landings on some makeshift aircraft carriers about two or three miles offshore. I thought I couldn't qualify, because I left school midway through my fourth year. Little did I realize that with the extra credits I had amassed, I had my diploma just for the asking. Unknown to me, my skipper on the submarine wrote to the school and had them send out two diplomas, one to my home and one to me on board. When the Captain handed me my diploma, I was shocked. He told me then that now I could apply for flight training, but since I was already in the submarine service I didn't pursue flying at that time. We had discussed my dream, but I didn't know he would go that far for me. Captain Nichols was from a Navy family generations deep.

Son Neil, lost to us in a tragic move when thirty-one years old, was born to fly. He had me all excited to fly also, but at that point I didn't have the time, nor the funds. At age 58, I was able to do it right. What a glorious feeling to be up in the air, free as a bird, getting rid of all the tension of the business world. Flying came as second nature to me. Purchasing the book of questions, with multiple tricky answers, I studied that book and passed the test with flying colors (pardon the pun). Actually, flying is very easy. Safety is what one most hone in on. I went to Howell Airport at 131st and Cicero Avenue in Crestwood, Illinois, for flight training. I was truly amazed when, after just about one-half hour of instructions, my instructor cut me loose. With his vigilance, he had me do three touch-and-go's, and then he got out of the plane and told me to do it solo. It was very thrilling for me to get my student pilot license so fast. I flew every day, mostly for pleasure, but some for business. I would make a lunch date with a client in Wisconsin, rent a plane at Midway Airport, fly up to Wisconsin for lunch, and be back by two or three o'clock.

Usually, my meetings would be at Delavan, Wisconsin. But as time progressed, I started traveling further within the ten-state area, from Nebraska to Ohio, Minnesota to Tennessee. Since I was not instrument rated, I especially was very careful to check the weather factor many times a day. I made it a rule not to fly in dubious weather, nor even if I consumed even one beer. "Eight hours from bottle to throttle" is the flier's criteria, and I firmly believed in adhering to that policy. Safety can be a two-way street. On landing at Howell, I had the nose gear collapse, and I came to rest with my wingtip just inches from a friend's garage. No damage except to the nose gear and my heart.

Returning from a meeting in Wausau, Wisconsin, I was about ten miles west of the Milwaukee airport when I specifically contacted that airport asking to be notified of any aircraft in the vicinity. A few minutes later, a Lear Jet veered off my nose. I contacted the airport, screaming at them, but they, sheepishly, wouldn't respond. Night flying is beautiful. On the same trip, I was inbound to land at the Frankfort, Illinois airport. A plane was sitting adjacent to the runway. Since I had announced my every move on the radio, I assumed the aircraft sitting there was waiting for me to land. WRONG. Almost at the point of no return, he swung onto the runway in front of me, and I had to abort the landing. He must not have had his radio on or he certainly would have heard my choice of names I called him. I was glad that trip was over.

Sister Alvernia of the Felician Sisters called me one day, asking if I would fly to Centralia, Illinois, to bring back Sister Lou Marie (my music teacher). She could not take the long car ride because of her health condition. There is nothing I nor my father wouldn't do for "our" Felicians. I immediately rented an RG Cessna (retractable gear).

The weather was perfect, a bright and sunny day. None of the nuns had ever been in a small plane before. I put Sister Lou Marie in front with me so she could take in the sights better, and two nurse nuns in the rear. It was a very nice trip. As I approached the airport, I could see the ambulance at the west end of the airport, waiting for us as planned. When the two nurse nuns switched Sister Lou Marie into the ambulance, they boarded my plane for the return trip. Since we had no time for lunch northbound, I landed at Bloomington and we had lunch there. I had a daughter at school there, so I knew the food was good there. Back in the air, the rest of the trip down was uneventful. With the nuns back home, I had my aircraft serviced. While refueling, I listened to the pilots talk about their close calls, never imagining I might be in the same position with a problem very soon.

Flying at 8,000 feet over Bloomington, Illinois, while talking to the air traffic controllers on the ground, all my electronics left me. This is a first for me. Can I do it? Of course I can. I'm sure the Felicians are praying for me. What more do I need?

How do I know my landing gears are down? There is a hydraulic pump to pump that should bring them down. But they didn't come down. Shaking the plane could bring them down, but shaking didn't do it either. Flying over Midway at 1,500 feet and looking for a signal, red or green, to either land or scoot out of the way, I got the red, so I headed south for Howell. Another decision to contemplate: Howell gave me three options, a grass runway, a cornfield in the center of the airport, or the cement runway. All the while I am pumping the hydraulic pump, hoping to see the landing gears, but NO LUCK. I then proceeded to use all safety procedures, coming in for a landing on the grass, aborting at the last second. I did the same thing on the cornfield.

Now I am down to my last option, the cement runway. Just as I am about to land, the left landing gear shook loose. I assumed the right one was down though I couldn't visually see it. I again aborted the landing, for I didn't know if the nose wheel was down. Not knowing for sure, and not knowing of any other procedure that would give me total assurance that it was down. I decided to make a soft wheel landing (land on back wheels and gently lower the nose). What a relief when that maneuver worked! I found a pay phone and called the rental agent to come and get his plane. I told him that none of the electronics worked and that I was NOT going to fly this plane in that condition. Imagine my surprise when the owner of the plane called me to thank me for not damaging his aircraft. It seems he had no insurance on it. Later on I found that people sometimes lease out their aircraft to agents who are supposed to insure them but don't.

A niece in our family, long ago, was injured in an auto accident, taking an airplane as her settlement. She later lost it by some agent not insuring it, and having it be involved in an air accident.

GAMBLING

One day I looked in the paper and saw an ad in the Tribune talking about free passes to and from Las Vegas, no charge at all, on the red-eye special. Leave O'Hare field at 5:00 p.m, come back at 6:00 or 7:00 a.m. So I tried it. In fact, in did it five times and I didn't bet a nickel, but I asked a lot of questions at the craps table and I thought I had a good background, so the sixth time I went to Vegas I bet slowly, small amounts, and I was successful. I was successful three times in a row to begin with, so I thought, well, I'll make the stakes a little higher, so I used a little more of their money and it kept growing and growing. Finally I became a favorite at the Frontier Hotel. They had me golfing with the pros six or seven times; that alone would have cost about four thousand dollars to enter the field, but it was all comped, all free. All I could eat, all I could drink, free board, beautiful hotel room.

And as we progressed, as I got more proficient, finally we were invited to Hawaii, 90 couples. We got to Las Vegas on Saturday. Saturday night they had a luau for us with every type of seafood you could imagine. We each got our own name-embroidered-on-terrycloth bathrobe. And the next morning, Sunday, we flew to Hawaii, 90 couples. They put a bottle of our favorite whiskey in front of us; of course that didn't set well with my children's mother. That night, before leaving, I won six thousand dollars and I gave it to her and she thought we'd have to give it back; she was a real negative person. In any event, we spent the week in Hawaii. Beautiful weather. I golfed again. Didn't even know I won money until we got back to Vegas. Come back to Las Vegas for the weekend and we went our separate ways. My airfare was paid all the way, and hers. It was great. The Frontier Hotel treated me very, very well.

I had made a gambling contact in Chicago, who handled all my gambling reservations on a moment's notice. The only time he failed me was actually my fault. I made a split second decision to take Kay to Puerto Rico for a weekend. He was going on a vacation himself, so he left the arrangements to be made by his secretary. Things went from bad to worse. Upon arrival, first of all, there was no limo to greet me, so we had to take a cab to the Sands Hotel. This did not set too well with me since I was so spoiled by the attention I was accustomed to getting. I did have a suite reserved, which was very beautiful, but there was another disappointment when the gambling arrangement was discussed. I had quite a bit of their money, but my credit line was in dispute. This was Friday evening and the boss of the gambling concession was gone for the day. I then told the clerk that we would enjoy their hospitality but we would not gamble unless my terms were met. To get to our suite, we had to pass through a room full of exotic foods, drinks, absolutely out of this world. Since it was late Friday, the usual server was gone, so a note indicated we should take whatever we wanted to our room. Our room was at ground level with its own small refrigerator full of goodies. Kay, being a pineapple freak, found a can of pineapple juice showing "bottled" in Puerto Rico.

This took care of our plans to tour the island on Saturday. Sorry to say, the pineapple fields were blocked from view by car, so we were content to just travel while I showed her places of contact for my business. The main hotel I wanted her to see was the El

Conquistador, where every room had an ocean view. Another feature of this beautiful hotel was a swimming pool at several layers with a tram to take in the view on the way down to the beach. Unfortunately, the hotel was closed; bankrupt, if you will.

The main point I wanted to show Kay was the main dining room. Its color motif was purple and black. To enter, one had to cross a bridge over water, and that room was uniquely "decorated" with wood scraps from the construction, all nailed to the walls in helter-skelter fashion, painted purple. It really was "different". The coup de gras was the seating throughout, everything done in purple. Some ingenuity was called into play here. Picture yourself sitting on one-half a VW (auto), or one-half a rowboat, to eat dinner. Quaint to say the least, wouldn't you say?

Still burned up over the lack of my usual and expected treatment, I booked us into a show or two while relaxing Sunday. I finally did hear from the Sands that my wishes were granted, and my credit line was what I said it was supposed to be. This being Sunday evening, and since we were planning on leaving early Monday morning, I decided to return the rental car. Unfortunately, I did gamble earlier that Sunday, not in my usual fashion, falling behind $5,800. Kay was in bed as I left to return the rental. I told her I would return the car and pick up my airfare and go to the craps table. Usually, they would give me cash, but this time they gave me chips. I asked Kay for her "lucky" number, and she picked eight. To make a long story short, I won back my losses ($5,800), won an additional $2,400, won $2,100 on the number eight for Kay, so things were getting rosier by the minute. Not ten feet away, I heard the bells ringing for someone who had hit a jackpot on the slot machine. Turning around, there was Kay, blushing because she didn't like the attention the ringing bells gave her. So, we were leaving on a high positive note the next morning. When offered a limo to take us to the airport, I declined, letting the man in charge know that he would be hearing from my Chicago contact.

While I did not win every time, being far ahead, I governed my losses so that I at least received the benefits of their hospitality.

When golfing with the pros I was allowed to bring along a caddy. Rich Mikalik was my caddy, and he and I reveled in the food that they put before us. The Frontier hired Hollywood women to keep our plates full and drinks coming. Everything was done first class. I certainly will never forget golfing with Al Geiberger, Arnold Palmer, Orville Moody, the Edwards brothers, and so many others.

When I was attempting to keep the SILVERSIDES submarine in Chicago, I prevailed upon many casinos in Las Vegas to donate for the cause. Only one did, and that was the Frontier. John Miner was the manager of the Frontier's casino, and I eventually considered him to be a good friend of mine; he later moved over to the Stardust to be the general manager there. Before making that move, he brought a group from Las Vegas to Chicago and I gave them a tour of the SILVERSIDES. "Everything happens for the best," my personal motto, still goes, for she is now domiciled in Muskegon, Michigan, where hopefully she'll be for years and years to come.

I took my cousin's husband "Skinny" to the Bahamas on an overnight junket where he proved to be the world's worst poker player. While I was winning at craps, he kept coming back for more and more chips. But he had fun, and so did I. It would be most difficult to put a price tag on his friendship. He was a fierce competitor on the golf course, bowling, or doing anything requiring competition. EXCEPT POKER.

FUN TIMES

Wisconsin Vacation. Thanks to earlier associations with Stanley Steffke and family, who ran FOREWAY EXPRESS in Wisconsin, we, Chicago-Miami, became their agents in Chicago. Prior to that marriage, they could only go as far as the Illinois border, as their rights dictated. I was well aware of all the Wisconsin cities and towns from my soliciting for Armellini Express. One of Foreway's road drivers heard me talk about taking my family on vacation into northern Wisconsin, and offered to let us use his summer cottage free. He drew us a map, very accurate, by the way, with handwritten instructions which we followed with no trouble. Once there, we found the key exactly where he said it would be. Following his written instructions, we turn the water on, by first picking up the pump cover. By this time, being deep in the woods, we noticed the too numerous bees, mosquitoes, and most of all, GNATS. We didn't even need to vote. We all pitched in and reversed our efforts and ran out of those woods.

We ended up renting a nice clean (no gnat) cottage at a place called the Waldell Resort, where we stayed and enjoyed swimming, waterskiing, etc. A nice-looking lady from the next cottage just had her hair done when Paul came in on skis and splashed her but good. After that, she watched for Paul and ran for cover when he started coming in.

One trick old Dad pulled on the kids was to take them in our van to the garbage dump. I would tell them to be ultra quiet. Putting on my headlights, you could see bears rooting through the garbage. Parking on a slight incline, I would release the brakes and tell them a bear was pushing us. Needless to say, this terrorized them.

It was a nice vacation, especially considering the terrible start. I don't think that I told the man the truth about us not using his cottage. I can't help but wonder how he and his family stood those gnats.

CANADA ONE.

At Magician Lake one day, three boys got together and made a decision. Paul Bocian, Mike Rekruciak, and Jeff Derda decided that they were going to take their fathers on a Canadian fishing trip. On the specified date (1974), we headed for the boundary waters of Canada. We rented three canoes, parked our car, and headed northward with our supplies. I had Paul as my "motor," making it easy for me as my only job then was to steer. Two of our canoes kept a straight line, but the third didn't for lack of experience, I suppose. We did have a great time, regardless.

We had to portage a lot, since the lakes were of different heights, and we had to work around the wooden dams. One day, while in our camp, seven canoes passed by, each with three women in them. They kept a firm line and a brisk pace, too. We met up with them a day or two later at a portage point. The Derdas were in the lead pulling up at the portage point. Jeff turned towards us (Bocians and Rekruciaks were bringing up the rear), yelling what we thought was "BEARS". In reality, in front of them were these 21 ladies sunning themselves in the all-together. By the time Paul and I showed up, the girls were decently covered up. We ended up camping just a mile or two beyond them, and set out fishing that area. In a short while, the seven canoes came by in perfect single file. Of course, Jeff and Mike and Paul found out who they were and how often they took these trips, etc. Leave it to the younger generation. The girls took these trips yearly, having formed some sort of club.

This trip with our sons turned out to be one of the best vacations of our lives. I'm glad we had Paul along, for the very primitive maps given to us by the Canadians needed his Viet Nam experience as we entered every new lake. He would take one look at the map and point to where he "knew" the next portage place was.

BEST SEATS IN CUBS PARK.

My nephew Bill Allen, my son Garry and I went to a Cubs-White Sox game at Wrigley Field. We sat in the first row behind the dugout, at a point where the players had to come right at us before stepping down into the dugout. To the right of us were two young men who were season ticket holders. Though obviously Cubs fans, you couldn't tell by the way they vilified Sammy Sosa. This was a short time after Sosa was caught with the cork in his bat as it broke for all the world to see. Of course, his new name became Corky. The two young men to our right were less cordial than that, as their names for him are unprintable. Sosa was visibly shaken every time he returned to the dugout. Most Cubs fans that we saw and heard were NOT behind him one bit. As a Sox fan, I loved it, but as a former baseball player, I felt sad that it happened, as it cheapened his home run records in my estimation. We will never know how much it helped him, or for how long he was using those cork-filled bats.

As a youngster, I must have filled at least ten or more scrapbooks with newspaper clippings of sports figures and related data. I could recite all players' names, records, no matter which team they played for. I somehow misplaced an almanac I once had that showed Sox/Cubs having played a city series much like the

World Series is played today. To the best of my recollection, the Sox won 19 of 25, and most of those years, the Sox were very low in the standings and the Cubs high. This would be games before the 1940s. I showed those facts to Cubs fans every chance I got. I sure wish I had those scrapbooks today.

SWITZERLAND

Some years back, our square dance group, about sixteen of us strong, took a trip to Switzerland. I purchased a new Bell & Howell camera which recorded voice as it shot pictures, so that the narration enhanced everything. I shot twenty-five magazines of film, thinking I had a lot of memories of the trip captured forever. When I sent the film in, I was thoroughly disappointed. All the film came back totally dark. It seems that the automatic exposure malfunctioned and ruined all the film. Bell & Howell did give me twenty-five new magazines, but that hardly compensated for my treasured pictures. They were moving pictures, so nothing short of duplicating the trip in person could make up for my loss, and they certainly weren't willing to pay for that.

Some priceless shots were taken from the tour guide's seat as we negotiated hairpin turns in the Swiss Alps. I traded seats with the guide. The motor coach had the front wheels considerably recessed, so that halfway through the turn, one could actually look down and see a thousand foot drop underfoot as the front of the coach made the turn.

Taking a cog railway trip up to the Jungfrau was a thrill. Actually, we rode the tram halfway up, and the cog railway the rest of the way. At the top there was an ice castle. It was treacherous footing, but very interesting to see the rooms sculpted out of ice. The view was breathtaking. On the return tram trip, we passed over cows feeding on the mountainside. They were eyeing us as we came very close to their heads.

The tram I refer to is the ski-lift mechanism. This being summertime, the lifts came in handy for tourism. INTERLOCHEN is a town "between the lakes." It seems our tour guide told us what Interlochen meant every few minutes. One thing of interest is the Swiss coffee servings. Their "cup" of coffee is the size of a good-sized American soup bowl.

We visited a clockmaker's shop which had hundreds of clocks with quaint faces. It was named, quite appropriately, the William Tell. This shop was on a hillside, on the second floor, and we were lucky enough to catch their noontime movement of cows, each one having a bell attached to it for their farmer's recognition. Each cow also had a pretty bow fastened to its head.

Square dancers do "fun" things much like the Boy Scouts. They "earn" patches, and we earned several unique ones on this trip. One was for dancing in the restrooms. Another was for dancing in four different countries on the same day. Those countries were Switzerland, Germany, Lichtenstein, and Austria.

At our hotel, someone had a yen for wine, so I was chosen to go out and purchase the wine. Since our hotel was on the border of Austria and Switzerland, I leisurely walked into Austria looking for a liquor store. Not knowing the language, and not knowing I was in any danger (I later found out I was), I walked into a gala party of Austrians having a grand time. I found a person who spoke English, and danced a polka with a well-endowed gal at his request. It was then he told me the danger of walking the dark streets of Austria, especially at the border. He also found me a magnum of wine to take back to my group at the hotel. I was tempted to stay at the party.

Before entering too far into Germany for our dancing, our guide pointed out the dozens of houses of ill repute lining both sides of the street. This was not allowed by the Swiss government, so Germany took full advantage of this. Our guide was quick to point out that most of the "girls" at these places came from Switzerland to "earn" a living.

Grand Canyon trip, 1976. In 1976, I met a pilot of a tourist company and made a deal with him. I had us booked for a Grand Canyon raft trip in June, and he agreed to garage our new Cadillac while he flew us to Page, Arizona to start our raft trip. He then was scheduled to pick us up at Peach Springs after our trip and bring us to the Frontier Hotel in Las Vegas. The river trip was awesome. Every bend in the river brought a spectacular view. Sunday was our departure date, and I was out of film by midweek. Our guides were terrific, giving us historic data on the formation of the canyon, animal life, etc. We did side trips into some of the gorges, saw a village inhabited by the Havasupai tribe, and also saw waterfalls that were unbelievably beautiful deep in this arid place.

The pace of the river flow was governed by how much electricity was needed in the cities and towns serviced by the Glen Canyon Dam. When bedding down for the night, I was in charge of tying up our raft. There was brush and small tree stumps to tie into, but I learned a lesson the first night. I had to use fifty-foot lengths of rope to tie up properly a long way from the river's edge. This, because the river would rise overnight to take care of the electricity needs mentioned earlier. After that first night, I was given an "A" for my tying-up job.

On more than one occasion, we encountered rattlers, who slithered away upon our arrival. The guides said to stay out of their way and they will stay out of yours. We walked six miles up one canyon to see a most beautiful set of waterfalls dropping into five cascading pools. At the very top of the pools, my son Neil and the other teens on our raft were jumping off a fifty-foot ledge, running back up, and jumping again.

Lava Falls was the culmination of our trip down the Colorado River through the Grand Canyon. We negotiated dozens of white water rapids in our rafts (there were two rafts in our group), most being very timid and mild. We looked forward to the granddaddy of them all, Lava Falls. It was the last and most vicious of all the falls we were to encounter.

Before going through the falls, we pulled over to the shore and watched as other rafters negotiated them. Our guide wanted us to see what we were going to be going through before we did it ourselves. Right in the middle of the rapids arose a huge stone. It would take the skill of our guides to properly hit that stone at a glancing blow, not to have people falling overboard, along with all our provisions and gear. We watched a group of six or seven small, two-man boats (each with a schoolteacher and a guide with the exception of one lone schoolteacher) go down, some losing their oars, some tossing persons out of their boats, none of them getting through without mishap. Lastly came the lone woman in the last boat, and we all cheered her on from our perches on land. She did a perfect job of it, to the disbelief of all of us watching.

Now came our turn. Everyone running the rapids, by law, had to have life vests on at all times. Rangers were everywhere, checking that we all had vests on. In fact, we were delayed at the start of our trip by a ranger who wouldn't pass one of our group until her vest was exchanged for one that had all the fasteners working. We made the falls due to our expert guides, and spent the rest of the day leisurely heading downriver as there would be no more white water to negotiate. Lava Falls is about a sixty-foot drop in about a quarter of a mile. We would spend the final night camping, washing up, and sprucing up for our victorious return to the Frontier Hotel.

My wife was very thorough. She planned all our clothes by the day, even to the last day when we would be checking back into the Frontier Hotel in Las Vegas. Since our pilot was to pick us up at Peach Springs, Arizona, for the flight back to Las Vegas, all six of us had our cleanest clothes on. (I forgot to give the rundown on who the six of us were: Chris and Marv, Janine and Neil, Lou and I.) When the bus came down to the river's edge where we patiently waited, we all had our dirty clothes in plastic bags, sporting our clean duds. SURPRISE, all preparations were for naught. Our bus was an old school bus with no air conditioning, it was stifling hot so all the windows were open wide, and the eighteen miles of road we had to traverse were the dustiest, dirtiest one could imagine.

By the time we got to Las Vegas and checked into the Frontier, we looked like Buddy Ebsen's family checking into Hollywood after striking oil. Needless to say, we almost plugged up the bathtubs with sand and dust from our trip.

At breakfast the morning after returning to Las Vegas, Janine told me she saw Joe DiMaggio. I felt so proud of a daughter of mine recognizing a major league player, until she told me he was MR. COFFEE. The Frontier hosted a lot of Hollywood dignitaries, and my kids thought that was great. On one trip there, Rich Mikalik and I talked at great length with former Cub Ernie Banks. Another time, there alone, I had nice discussions with Joe Louis when he was their spokesman. Nothing would replace the memories of golfing with the pros. It was exhilarating and made me feel special.

Turning down the many offers for free trips to Monaco, Australia, Alaska and Hong Kong was hard to do.

NOTRE DAME, MY HEROES

Garry and I were invited to a Notre Dame game against Boston College. Our friends from South Bend, Indiana and Magician Lake arranged a beautiful day for us. The Benassi's had a summer home near ours, and our kids played with theirs, almost 24/7. They "lived" on playing basketball on the court I made on my adjacent lot. I even rigged up a pair of spotlights high up in the trees, with the on/off switch in the house. That proved to be a stroke of genius on my part, for the kids didn't know that us grownups needed our sleep, so more than once I had to "darken" their domain. The day of the game, they had a friend through whom they could sneak in any number of cars in the Notre Dame parking lot to tailgate. They supplied the food, and frozen drinks made with a kind of gelatin. Not having any tickets in hand, I started to get a bit panicky, but was told not to worry, five minutes to game time and they will be giving tickets away free, AND THEY WERE. We had good seats, too.

Notre Dame was losing, so Garry and I decided to head for the Benassi's. On the car radio, we heard Notre Dame went ahead by two points. We entered the house just as Boston College was lining up to kick a field goal. As luck would have it, they made it good and Notre Dame lost by a point. I am a Notre Dame fan, win or lose.

noise, and he would turn and lumber further away. I didn't sleep well that night.

Carnival Cruise Lines, sometimes in the 1980's. We took this cruise along with about seven other couples from our square dance club. I have to admit it was fun. The cruise line provided entertainment galore, and we were with a fun group.

There came an announcement on the PA system that the Olympics were soon to start, but there were openings to be filled. Teams were to consist of five people, two women/girls and three men/boys. I tried to get some of our group to go with me to sign up, and apparently they were too bashful. When I got there they had only one opening, and the boys were strapping husky guys who looked at my belly saying to themselves, "Look what we got". I put aside their silent complaints, and proceeded to win (for the team) the first "game," which was jump rope. Not having skipped rope since I was about ten, I did very well, while my two "boys" bumbled and fumbled away clumsily, so they brightened up when I won that event. Next was a dribbling contest, which was a bit more difficult as the ship was rolling, but I won that, too. Again, the smiles on their faces told me they were glad to have me on their team. There were five events total, and I won four of them. I lost the last one for the team, as it was a measurement of the girth of all of us, and while the rest of the team were all slim jims, my belly lost it for us.

We did get the gold medals, and the band played our national anthem. Our square dancers cheered us on but they were sorry they didn't accompany me when I asked them to. Carnival Lines was the finest cruise I took, and I would recommend them highly.

GOLF TOURNAMENT

On August 30, 1984, I participated in a golf tournament sponsored by Andy Williams. All participants were former professional athletes and I was on a gambling junket in Atlantic City, New Jersey, at the Sands Hotel. When asked if I wished to participate, naturally I accepted. Getting a hole in one couldn't have been further from my mind. I have been close on many occasions, but this day I did get one. My excitement was twofold. Watching his sponsored tourneys on TV, I saw golfers get beautiful exotic cars like Mazerattis or some such vehicle. What was I to get? Really, actually, NOTHING. I saw next to Mr. Williams at the banquet, and mentioned the hole in one. He said, "What did you get?" I told him "Nothing." Some two or three weeks later I did get a TV set. I had quite an impressive list of witnesses, such as Larry Doby, Elroy Face, Pete Mahavlich, Lenny Moore, all, of course, past their prime at the time. Anyone getting a hole in one is supposed to buy the house a drink. Since I was a freebie, everything was gratis, so I took over the mike and told the bartenders to give everyone a drink. Easy to play big shot under those conditions.

The tourney was at the Great Bay Golf Club, about twenty miles northwest of Atlantic City. They did give me a pair of shoes, several golf gloves, two golf shirts, and other items. All combined, they did fall short of the sports car. I went home thinking I really accomplished something rare. About a year later, they sent me a book which deflated my ego. This book listed all of the holes in one for the year, the total being about six thousand. It showed the date, the place, the hole, the length of the hole. So there was my name all right, in amongst the thousands of others. Of course, I cherish the fact that I did get one. I understand some pros do not have one, while others have over thirty. So much for golf.

Grand Canyon Trip, 1986. In 1985, we booked a year in advance a most memorable hike from the South Rim to the North Rim, a total of about 21 miles.

The trip really began with a request from our dear Felician Nuns to bring back a truckload of their belongings from a convent in the St. Louis area. Since we (eight of us) would be passing through St. Louis in our motor home, we executed the plan of all plans.

We drove one of my trucks, as well as the motor home, dropping off the truck for the Sisters to load while we went on to our hiking Grand Canyon trip in the motor home and would pick up the truck on the way back. The nuns did such a great job of loading it that I wished they worked for me.

With many drivers, we pushed right on through to the South Rim, where we slept the night. We knew we would need walking sticks, so what did we do? We went to a hardware store and purchased eight mops, threw away the mopheads, and used the blue mop handles for our walking sticks. WE WERE READY. Knowing we had a delicious steak dinner awaiting us at the Phantom Ranch at our half-way point at the bottom of the Canyon, we grabbed a light breakfast and away we went.

Being the elder statesman, I was privileged not to have to carry a heavy backpack. Instead, I carried two gallons of water to start with. My load became lighter as we progressed and each kept coming to me for more and more water. The hikers really looked like they were enjoying it, as every switchback, every descent brought about a more spectacular view. The immensity of the Canyon made one feel very much in awe.

Part-way down, while we rested in the only place one could find shade, a voice from someone following us rang out calling my nephew's name. Can you imagine recognizing someone's voice in so remote a place as the Grand Canyon? It was a school chum of Bob Caffarella. Besides my nephew Bob, our group consisted of my son Garry and his father-in-law, Carl Mueller, my son Paul, his friend Kelly Wachholz, my daughter Chris and her husband Marvin, and myself. The KAIBOB trail going down had no waterfalls, just desert-like conditions all the way. I thought I had good hiking boots. Unfortunately, the foot movement with each step caused me to lose two large toenails; but that's another story.

The trail down was far from easy, especially with signs all along indicating that the mule trains got preference. Signage stated for hikers to move to the outer edge of the trail when a mule train passed by. That's one rule we flat refused to abide by. The Phantom Ranch was a most welcome sight, with its air conditioned sleeping quarters and the beautiful steak dinner served there. Once in my bed, I couldn't budge until we were to start our upward hike to the North Rim the next morning. That trail was wider, and had waterfalls in several places, where some of our gang would go to "shower" themselves. Not I.

At about the half-way point, we set up camp for the night. I was so tired, I laid down my bedroll with a rock right in the middle of my back and wouldn't or couldn't remove it. I don't know if it was my imagination or whatever, but I thought I awoke at one time of night with a mule deer snorting in my face. They were plentiful, so it is quite possible. Upon reaching the North Rim, we kissed the ground. Our friend, Reed Schulz, who had driven the motor home around the horn from south to north, was there with his plane. While the remainder of the gang prepared to return via St. Louis, Chris, Marv and myself were taken on an aerial trip the length of the Canyon, and then on to Phoenix.

About a hundred feet above the river, on the front porch, is a tee, some golf balls, and a few clubs. Down below is a green to aim at, a real challenge as it only measures about fifteen feet square. When the supply of golf balls is exhausted, someone has to take the walk down with a bucket to retrieve all the errant shots. Straight down to the green would only be about 150 feet. However, one must take the road, which increases the distance to about a quarter of a mile. I know, because that's the penalty for using up the last of the ball supply. Ovelia fit in perfectly.

MISCELLANEOUS

CDL – Citizens for Decent Literature – a very important part of my life. Very close friends of mine asked me join them in their fight against pornography and obscenity. Led by a very sainted priest, Father F. X. Lawlor, this group went into full swing, determined to make a dent in the pornographic world. It meant giving up living as we once knew it, and complete dedication to the cause. The men went out every night giving talks to church groups, while the wives appeared in court to show the judges they cared. Illinois had a good law which we utilized in trying to stem the tide, and we did have a 96% conviction rate on those we brought to trial. We were doing fine, until the Supreme Court reversed nineteen of our convictions, and we lost the impetus. A publishing company filed a suit against us, saying they would cancel the suit if we quit fighting. We continued, and had some high and mighty lawyers behind us. In order to pay our fees, which were only one-third of the going rate, I ran yearly dances as fund raisers. Thanks to the Supreme Court, we eventually had to throw in the towel.

Bill Schulz, one of our original group, had just moved to the suburbs where several of our group had also moved. His "move" was not really even started, as there was no furniture moved in but one sofa. As the last dance concluded, I thanked the crowd (over eleven hundred people) and invited them to Bill's house. Thirty-five showed up, some with lunchmeats and bread, some with drinks. It was a ball. Funnier yet, it had been a long-standing joke that Bill had told his son Richard that they would move out and not tell him where to. Richard returned from Viet Nam to his former Chicago home, only to find it empty. Richard's mail apparently didn't reach him in time, so the poor outcast didn't know where to turn. He managed to find them somehow, evidently through some kind neighbors. The Schultz family were great friends to have. Bill was the ultimate storyteller; unfortunately, in 2007 he passed away in Phoenix, where he and wife Althea had retired to.

Bill and Althea were invited to our Magician Lake home one winter weekend. On arrival, Bill rang the doorbell, and when I answered, he asked, "Is this the Bocian summer home?" He then proceeded to go back to his trunk, pulled out a golf club and a black golf ball, and hit it out onto the frozen lake. After that, with no words, he put back the club and acted like nothing happened. Bill drank tea at that time. Once inside our house, he walked right into the kitchen area, opened a cabinet door, and pulled out a used tea bag that he had hidden there on a previous visit.

I was given the honor of giving Richard's wife away (to Richard, of course) at their marriage. I can still hear her screaming when I arrived with my bowling shoes on, covered with multi-colored round stickers, saying I didn't have any other shoes to wear. Judy took it like a fall guy.

While golfing with Bill, my pull-cart fell apart. Bill offered to go get me a new one since he was riding due to his heart condition. I was doing quite well, so I elected to carry my clubs the remainder of the game. Bill found a round heavy rock which he felt I might need for our Michigan home. I told him there was a stone quarry less than a mile away, so I didn't need it. Carrying my clubs, approaching the 18th green, he asked me for his five iron, as did another member of our group. This was a hot, muggy day, and I unknowingly was carrying extra clubs, PLUS THAT ROCK.

What to do to get even? I had a van, and loaded a round boulder weighing at least 75 pounds in it. The Schulz family lived near my home, so I conveniently dropped off the stone, blocking their storm door, and rang their bell and ran away. I know that he knew who left the stone, but he never once brought up the subject. Finally, one of my children couldn't stand it anymore and brought up the subject. He had the last laugh AGAIN.